24.95

W9-BVW-429

MIDDLE EAST NATIONS IN THE NEWS

Egypt
IN THE NEWS

PAST, PRESENT, AND FUTURE

Susan Jankowski

MyReportLinks.com Books

an imprint of

Enslow Publishers, Inc.

Box 398, 40 Industrial Road
Berkeley Heights, NJ 07922
USA

MyReportLinks.com Books, an imprint of Enslow Publishers, Inc. MyReportLinks®
is a registered trademark of Enslow Publishers, Inc.

Library of Congress Cataloging-in-Publication Data

Jankowski, Susan.
  Egypt in the news : past, present, and future / Susan Jankowski.
     p. cm. — (Middle East nations in the news)
  Includes bibliographical references and index.
  ISBN 1-59845-031-X
  1. Egypt—Juvenile literature. I. Title. II. Series.
  DT49.J35 2006
  962—dc22
                                        2005032438

Printed in the United States of America

10 9 8 7 6 5 4 3 2 1

To Our Readers:
Through the purchase of this book, you and your library gain access to the Report Links that specifically back up this book.
The Publisher will provide access to the Report Links that back up this book and will keep these Report Links up to date on **www.myreportlinks.com** for five years from the book's first publication date.
We have done our best to make sure all Internet addresses in this book were active and appropriate when we went to press. However, the author and the Publisher have no control over, and assume no liability for, the material available on those Internet sites or on other Web sites they may link to.
The usage of the MyReportLinks.com Books Web site is subject to the terms and conditions stated on the Usage Policy Statement on **www.myreportlinks.com.**
A password may be required to access the Report Links that back up this book. The password is found on the bottom of page 4 of this book.
Any comments or suggestions can be sent by e-mail to comments@myreportlinks.com or to the address on the back cover.

Photo Credits: Al Mashriq, p. 65; AP/Wide World Photos, pp. 1, 53, 87, 110; ArabNet, p. 51; BBC, pp. 12, 34, 46; Cable News Network, LP, LLLP, p. 105; Carnegie Museum of Natural History, p. 82; Christopher Rose, p. 85; CIA, pp. 6, 112; CNN Interactive, p. 44; © Corel Corporation, pp. 3, 6 (pyramids), 16, 18, 22–23, 32, 38, 42, 48–49, 60–61, 66–67, 70–71, 75, 84, 102; © Diamar, p. 8; Courtesy Jimmy Carter Library, p. 93; Egypt's Cabinet of Ministers, p. 95; Egypt State Information Service, p. 99; Embassy of Egypt, p. 14; Enslow Publishers, Inc., p. 5; IDSC, p. 78; InterCity Oz, Inc., p. 35; Library of Congress, pp. 55, 89; LOC Egypt, p. 108; Mike Dowling, p. 91; MSU EMuseum, p. 59; MyReportLinks.com Books, p. 4; National Geographic Society, p. 40; PBS, p. 80; Theban Mapping Project, p. 73; The British Museum, p. 63; The Egyptian Presidency, p. 10; The Official Web site of the Nobel Foundation, p. 57; The University of Chicago Library, p. 30; United Nations, p. 104; University of Texas Libraries, pp. 25, 28; U.S. State Department, p. 97; WN News Network, p. 20.

Cover Photo: AP/Wide World Photos

Cover Description: President Hosni Mubarak waves to supporters during his 2005 reelection campaign.

Contents

Mud-brick village

Egyptian guide

MyReportLinks.com Books
Great Books, Great Links, Great for Research!

The Internet sites featured in this book can save you hours of research time. These Internet sites—we call them *"Report Links"*—are constantly changing, but we keep them up to date on our Web site.

When you see this "Approved Web Site" logo, you will know that we are directing you to a great Internet site that will help you with your research.

Give it a try! Type http://www.myreportlinks.com into your browser, click on the series title and enter the password, then click on the book title, and scroll down to the Report Links listed for this book.

The Report Links will bring you to great source documents, photographs, and illustrations. MyReportLinks.com Books save you time, feature Report Links that are kept up to date, and make report writing easier than ever! A complete listing of the Report Links can be found on pages 114–115 at the back of the book.

Please see "To Our Readers" on the copyright page for important information about this book, the MyReportLinks.com Web site, and the Report Links that back up this book.

Please enter NEG1058 if asked for a password.

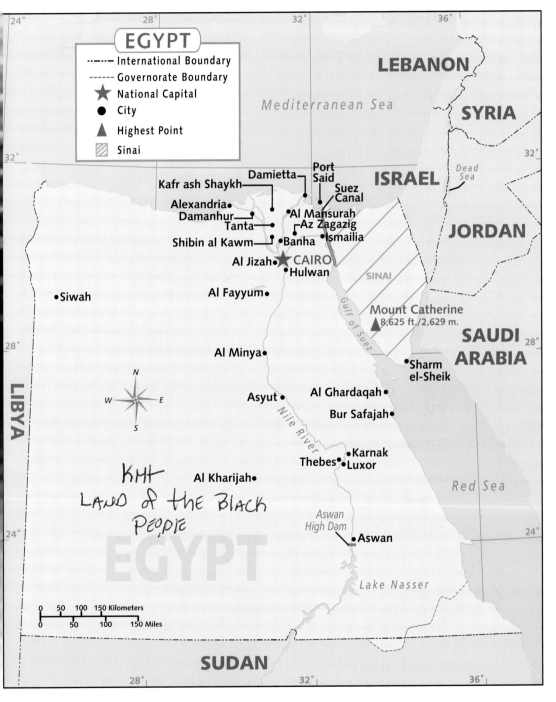

Map of Egypt

National Flag
Three equal horizontal stripes of red, white, and black. Red on top signifies overthrow of King Farouk before 1952; white for transition to independence without bloodshed; and black symbolizes the end of British colonial rule. Saldin's golden eagle at the center was originally a hawk, then changed to the larger bird.

Official Name
Arab Republic of Egypt

Capital
Cairo

Population
78.88 million people
(July 2006 estimate)

Area
386,559 square miles

Lowest Point
Qattara Depression,
436 feet below sea level

Highest Point
Mount Catherine,
8,625 feet

Government
Parliamentary

Head of State
President Mohammed Hosni Mubarak

Head of Government
Prime Minister Ahmed Nazif

Monetary Unit
Egyptian pound

Languages
Arabic (official), English, French

National Anthem
"My Homeland"

National Flower
Blue Water Lily

National Tree
Date Palm

Pyramids at Giza, Egypt.

Time Line

7000 B.C.	—Humans settle lands along the Nile River.
3000 B.C.	—Upper and Lower Egypt unites.
1500 – 1100 B.C.	—Pyramids and temples are built during the eighteenth through the twentieth dynasties.
600 – 500 B.C.	—Assyrian, Mesopotamian, and Persian conquests.
300 B.C.	—Alexander the Great founds Alexandria.
30 B.C.	—Queen Cleopatra's empire falls to Rome.
A.D. 642	—Arabs conquer Egypt; they convert people to Islam.
969	—Cairo becomes Egypt's capital city.
1100	—Saladin, Egypt's Sunni caliph, defeats Shi'ite Muslims and later Christian crusaders.
1250–1500	—The Mamluks rule Egypt.
1517	—Egypt becomes part of Turkish Ottoman Empire.
1798	—France invades Egypt but is defeated by the British.
1800	—Muhammed Ali takes control after conquering the Mamluks.
1869	—The Suez Canal is built.
1922	—Egypt gains internal independence from Great Britain under King Farouk I.
1928	—The Muslim Brotherhood is founded in Egypt.
1948	—Egypt joins other Arab nations in attacking Israel.
1952	—Gamal Abdel Nasser leads a coup against King Farouk and becomes prime minister to establish full independence from Britain.
1967	—Egypt joins other Arab countries in the Six-Day War with Israel and loses control of the Gaza Strip.
1970	—Assassination of President Nasser; Vice President Anwar Sadat is named successor.
1971	—Parliament creates a new constitution under Sadat's leadership.
	—The nation officially becomes the Arab Republic of Egypt.
1978	—Egypt and Israel sign the Camp David Peace Accords.
	—The Arab League expels Egypt. Sadat is assassinated a year later.
1981	—Hosni Mubarak becomes president by national referendum.
1989	—Egypt rejoins the Arab League.

Egyptian children

1995	—Mubarak is the target of an assassination attempt.
1997	—A terrorist attack at the Luxor Temple kills sixty tourists.
2001	—Egypt forms an agreement with Lebanon and Syria for a natural gas pipeline under the Mediterranean Sea.
2005	—A terrorist attack at the Red Sea resort town of Sharm El-Sheik occurs.
	—The Egyptian government opens elections to multiple political parties.
	—President Mubarak is reelected for a sixth term.
2006	—A passenger-cargo ferry sinks in Red Sea; one thousand die.

Chapter 1

Egypt Protects Centuries of Progress

Headline: EGYPTIAN DIPLOMAT KILLED BY KIDNAPPERS

BAGHDAD – An Egyptian embassy official in Iraq was killed five days after he was kidnapped near his Baghdad home. Ihad Al-Sherif was seized by terrorists while buying a newspaper on July 2, 2005. Then they videotaped his murder. He is survived by his family.

"Al-Sherif lost his life at the hand of terrorism that trades in the name of Islam, but knows no nation," the Egyptian government officially stated in its response to the news. Al-Qaeda terrorists have claimed responsibility for the killing.[1]

✯   ✯   ✯

The brutal crime is especially disturbing to world leaders. The United Nations (UN) also condemned Al-Sherif's murder. Egypt is among the Arab nations that are trying to support Iraq's new government without causing a backlash among extremists within their own borders. The murder of Al-Sherif is proof that terrorists are a threat to Muslims in Egypt and the Middle East, as well as people in the West.

The Egyptian government, headed by President Hosni Mubarak, does not support United States involvement in Iraq. At the start of the conflict, Mubarak said repeatedly that the United States Attack on Iraq is an attack on the Arab people. However, government officials and religious leaders have taken the official stance that it is proper for Egyptians to support the Iraqi peoples.[2]

Shortly after the kidnapping of Al-Sherif, extremists attacked diplomats from Bahrain and Pakistan. These men were in Iraq to open embassies, as well. Fortunately, these diplomats

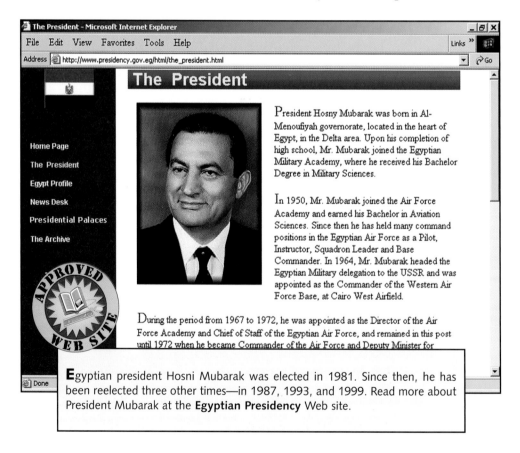

The President - Microsoft Internet Explorer

File   Edit   View   Favorites   Tools   Help   Links »

Address http://www.presidency.gov.eg/html/the_president.html   Go

The President

Home Page
The President
Egypt Profile
News Desk
Presidential Palaces
The Archive

President Hosny Mubarak was born in Al-Menoufiyah governorate, located in the heart of Egypt, in the Delta area. Upon his completion of high school, Mr. Mubarak joined the Egyptian Military Academy, where he received his Bachelor Degree in Military Sciences.

In 1950, Mr. Mubarak joined the Air Force Academy and earned his Bachelor in Aviation Sciences. Since then he has held many command positions in the Egyptian Air Force as a Pilot, Instructor, Squadron Leader and Base Commander. In 1964, Mr. Mubarak headed the Egyptian Military delegation to the USSR and was appointed as the Commander of the Western Air Force Base, at Cairo West Airfield.

During the period from 1967 to 1972, he was appointed as the Director of the Air Force Academy and Chief of Staff of the Egyptian Air Force, and remained in this post until 1972 when he became Commander of the Air Force and Deputy Minister for

Done

Egyptian president Hosni Mubarak was elected in 1981. Since then, he has been reelected three other times—in 1987, 1993, and 1999. Read more about President Mubarak at the **Egyptian Presidency** Web site.

survived. Currently, the United States military is fighting to establish a new government in Iraq after overthrowing Saddam Hussein, its former dictator.

Most Egyptians are Muslims who practice Sunni Islam. These individuals must balance traditional religious beliefs with Egypt's history of civil rights and technological advancement. Modern-day Egypt has its roots in ancient civilizations that thrived before the Islamic, Christian, and Jewish religions existed. Ancient Egypt was the longest-lived civilization of the ancient world.

However, violence by Islamic militants has threatened Egypt's stability in recent years, as well as the lives of its innocent citizens. The government has imposed strict policies to help maintain order during this period.

Ongoing State of Emergency

For over twenty years, Egypt has been under an official "state of emergency" declared by President Mubarak. This means that people have had to suspend certain civil rights to give Egyptian police more authority. Police have conducted "sweeps" in certain areas where terrorists are thought to be hiding. Hundreds of people have been arrested in these sweeps. Some believe this declaration was necessary to secure the safety of Egyptian citizens, as well as its leaders. Others have criticized

Egypt's president by saying the declaration only protects his own power over the nation's people.[3]

President Mubarak discussed a possible end to this state of emergency in his reelection campaign. He won his fifth term in office in 2005. But his political campaign did not always go smoothly. U.S. Secretary of State Condoleeza Rice visited President Mubarak prior to the election. She urged him to open the process to more candidates. The Egyptian parliament recently approved a constitutional amendment allowing more political parties to participate in elections.[4]

In 2005, Egypt held its parliamentary elections, which erupted in violence when opposition supporters claimed that Egyptian police were not allowing them to vote so as to protect the ruling NDP. The BBC provides more information on Egypt and its most recent elections at the **Country Profile: Egypt** Web site.

During President Mubarak's 2005 campaign, hundreds of protesters who opposed him were beaten by Egyptian plainclothes police in their attempts to control the crowds. The protesters want the state of emergency to end. Some also want to replace President Mubarak with a new leader.

Allies Against Terrorism

Although Egypt did not officially back the United States when it overthrew dictator Saddam Hussein in 2003, it supports Iraq's new government today. Hussein is accused of killing hundreds of thousands of ordinary Iraqi citizens. He is currently in custody and is on trial for massacres in his homeland.

Despite regional tensions, Egypt has worked with the United States and Israel in hunting down terrorists for the past twenty years. But Islamic extremists continue to use terrorism to try to stop Arab nations like Egypt from cooperating with Christians in the West, or Jews in Israel. They believe acts of violence will intimidate Muslim leaders like Mubarak and ultimately persuade him to support their political agenda.[5]

Yet Egypt remains eager to trade with the new, United States-backed Iraq. That country's oil reserves could provide for the fuel and energy needs of Egypt's 74 million residents. Although Egypt has some of its own oil, it is not enough to

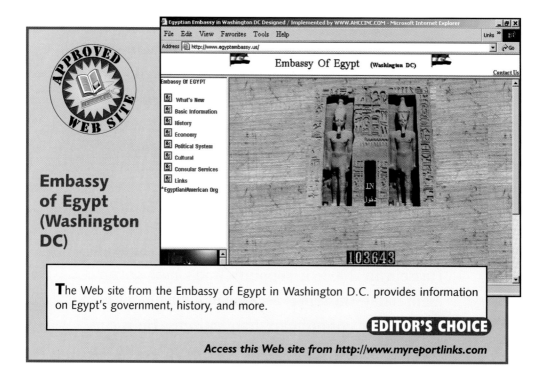

The Web site from the Embassy of Egypt in Washington D.C. provides information on Egypt's government, history, and more.

EDITOR'S CHOICE

Access this Web site from http://www.myreportlinks.com

meet its domestic needs. More recently, crude oil was discovered in the Nile River basin; however, the extent of resources in the basin is still under exploration. Egypt's primary involvement in the petroleum industry involves refining and shipping, as well as investments in oil companies. A trade agreement between Egypt and Iraq could benefit the economies of both countries. But following President Mubarak's reelection in 2005, the United States stalled trade talks to put pressure on Egypt to implement democratic, political reforms.[6]

In addition, Egypt is working with neighbors like Jordan and Israel to conserve natural resources and create new sources of energy.

Independent and sophisticated, Egypt is among the world's oldest civilizations. Today it has the largest population in the Middle East. It is the second most-populated country in Africa, after Nigeria. The majority of Egyptians live in the Nile River valley, which is lush, oasis land in the eastern part of the country. The Nile River is a historical trade route that has enabled Egypt to prosper for millennia. Its waters also helped Egyptians succeed at farming, which resulted in growth and prosperity for centuries.

Terrorists in Egypt

However, the Nile River also provided a passageway for Egypt's enemies. Thousands of years ago, the Egyptian armies established blockades at waterfalls and other Nile locations where there is rapid water flow, or cataracts. Egyptians used six cataracts to keep intruders from traveling upstream, as the Nile River flows from south to north. But their efforts to stave off intruders were not always successful. While Egyptians have been mighty conquerors, they have also been conquered themselves by enemies in the past.

In recent years, Egypt has had to hunt militants secretly operating on its own soil.[7] Today, terrorists are among Egypt's worst enemies. Some are members of an organization known as the Muslim Brotherhood, which has been outlawed in Egypt

⚠ *Located along the Nile River, Cairo is Egypt's largest city.*

and other countries. Members of this group murdered Egyptian officials during the 1990s. An Egyptian military court convicted six of these men of plotting to assassinate President Mubarak during his visit to Ethiopia in 1995. Security experts suspect corruption within Egypt's own military forces led to the murders and the plot on the president's life.[8]

▷ Toward Peaceful Coexistence

Three years later, Islamic terrorists killed sixty tourists at the landmark Luxor Temple. People from Japan and Europe, far removed from Middle Eastern politics, were among the victims. The Luxor killings affected Egypt's tourism industry because travelers want to feel safe when visiting another country. During this same period, ten civilians were gunned down in Cairo. Then, Egyptians who follow the Coptic sect of the Christian religion were labeled as "infidels" by Muslim extremists. They used this label to justify killing Copts in northern towns. Coptic Christians were persecuted in the past, but Mubarak's government protects religious freedoms.

The Arab Republic of Egypt is bordered by Jordan, a politically moderate country to its east; Sudan, an old, yet developing nation to its south; and Libya, a tribal Arab-African nation, to its west. Egypt's northern border forms much of the African coastline of the Mediterranean Sea. Israel borders Egypt to the far northeast. Despite the rise and fall of its many empires, Egypt also has a long history of peacefully coexisting with its neighbors. It is desperately trying to continue this pattern in modern times. But for modern Egypt, every alliance is risky.

Honoring a Treaty Amidst Turmoil

In summer 2005, Egypt honored its peace treaty with Israel by actively supporting the withdrawal of Jewish settlers from the Gaza Strip. Egypt had owned this land until Israel seized it during the

The Temple of Luxor is one of Egypt's most popular tourist attractions and was the target of a terrorist attack in 1998.

Arab-Israeli Six-Day War in 1967. Beginning in August, Jewish settlers were forced by the Israeli government to abandon their homes to make room for Palestinian people living near there.

After all the Jewish settlers had gone, hundreds of Palestinians stormed Egypt's border. Israel had restricted Palestinians' crossing of the Egyptian border for many years in an attempt to keep out weapons. After the Israeli settlers' withdrawal, some Palestinians crossed over into Egypt to reunite with relatives they had not seen for a long time. Others came to buy groceries, clothing, cigarettes, appliances, and other items, which are less expensive to buy in Egypt than in Israel. Still others crossed Egypt's border to escape violence and start new lives as immigrants. Both Jews and Palestinians had lived at odds with one another in different sections of Gaza since the Six-Day War. People on both sides endured frequent terror attacks on civilians in the Gaza Strip.

Although Egypt increased border security forces to stop crowds from entering, it was unable to prevent Palestinians from crossing in certain spots. Hundreds lined up for blocks to await their turn to try to cross into Egypt.

Israeli security officials fear that amidst this chaos, terrorists were able to smuggle guns and weapons into Gaza.

In early 2006, two people were trapped when a tunnel collapsed on the Egyptian border. Smugglers use these tunnels to bring everything from cigarettes to weapons into Gaza. The weapons could arm Hamas, the Palestinian militant group. Hamas was victorious as a political party in Palestine's first elections during this same period. Some members of Hamas proclaim Israel does not have the right to exist as a nation; they vow to destroy it. In the past, Hamas committed violent acts to pressure Israel into leaving Gaza and other areas, such as the West Bank near Jordan. Egypt is open to criticism from the international community for its failure to control the Palestinians at its border.

Updated on a daily basis, you will find the latest news from Egypt and the rest of the Middle Eastern region on the Egypt Daily Web site.

EDITOR'S CHOICE

Access this Web site from http://www.myreportlinks.com

Whether Egypt can stop illegal weapons trade between the two countries remains unclear.

In the midst of the Gaza withdrawal, a roadside bomb exploded near a vehicle transporting Canadian peacekeepers on the Sinai Peninsula. Fortunately, the two Canadians survived the attack. Less than one month earlier, Islamic militants exploded car bombs at the Red Sea resort of Sharm el-Sheik, which killed sixty-four tourists. In the wake of the explosions, Egyptian security forces found pickup trucks loaded with drugs and weapons. They are examining how the cars and trucks made it through Egypt's security checkpoints.

In summer 2005, Egyptian police arrested five suspected terrorists hiding on Halal Mountain, south of the Egyptian town of El Arish. In their pursuit, two Egyptian police officers died when land mines exploded on the mountain. Arab news media reported that officers Major General Mahmoud Adel and Lieutenant Colonel Omar Abdul Moneim were the highest-ranking policemen to lose their lives since four thousand Egyptian troops swept towns in northern Sinai in July 2005. That fall, Egyptian police caught a man involved in the bombings hiding in the nearby mountains.

To make matters worse, some international security experts suspect Islamic extremists are setting up terrorist operations in neighboring Sudan. In 2006, the U.S. Department of State

Sharm el-Sheik is Egypt's most widely visited resort area. Unfortunately, this resort was the target of a car bombing in 2006.

continued its official travel warning for people heading to Sudan. This type of unrest surrounds Egypt and has wide-reaching consequences. For example, instability has a negative impact on tourism, trade, and the economy. It also affects the quality of life for Egyptian people.

In addition to violence, modern Egypt is facing other problems. These include overpopulation, which leads to water and housing shortages; economic problems such as inflation and unemployment; and government bureaucracy, called red tape. There are political and military threats coming from both inside and outside the country. In the twenty-first century, this historical giant must meet modern challenges while preserving its much-celebrated history. Today, Egypt, the world's most ancient superpower, must secure the sands of its own cultural landscape.

Land and Climate

Headline: ISRAEL AND EGYPT TO BUILD NATURAL GAS PIPELINE

CAIRO – Egyptian and Israeli officials recently announced plans to build a natural gas pipeline that spans both countries. Officials endured summer heat and Cairo traffic to formalize the agreement on July 1, 2005. The agreement, signed by Egyptian oil minister Sameh Fahmy and Israeli infrastructure minister Binyamin Ben

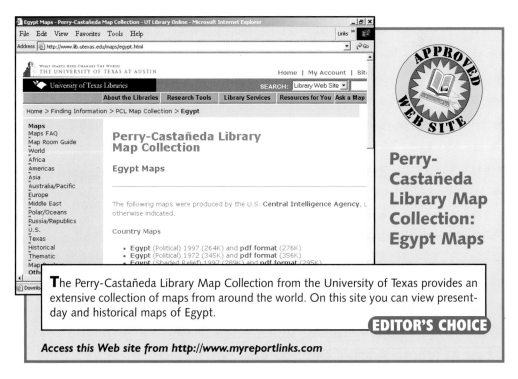

The Perry-Castañeda Library Map Collection from the University of Texas provides an extensive collection of maps from around the world. On this site you can view present-day and historical maps of Egypt.

EDITOR'S CHOICE

Access this Web site from http://www.myreportlinks.com

Eliezer, states Egypt will supply Israel with natural gas for fifteen years.

Leaders from the two nations used the occasion to emphasize their mutual cooperation. They say the $2.5 billion agreement is an example of the "solid peace" between Egypt and Israel since they signed the Middle East Peace Accord in 1979. Future plans for Egypt's natural gas supply could also involve new Palestinian companies in the Gaza Strip.[1]

☆   ☆   ☆

The pipeline will run parallel to the coastline of the Mediterranean Sea, close to offshore refining facilities. It will begin at El Arish on Egypt's Sinai Peninsula, south of Gaza, and end at Ashkelon in Israel, to the north. Construction is set to begin next year. The target date for completion is 2007. Israel recently vacated Gaza and gave control of the area to the Palestinians.

▷ Conserving Energy

The plan comes five years after Egypt formed an agreement with Lebanon and Syria to construct a natural gas pipeline under the Mediterranean Sea at a cost of one billion dollars. Natural gas is cheaper to produce than coal or other fossil fuels used to make electricity. It is also clean burning. This may help Egyptians and Israelis conserve energy and protect air quality in environments on both sides of their border.

Egypt has struggled to manage waste and pollution in its overcrowded cities for centuries. Beginning in the 1980s, the Egyptian Environmental Affairs Agency (EEAA) began establishing nature reserves known as Protected Areas. Over twenty of these parks exist throughout the country to preserve plant and animal species. For example, Protected Area breeding programs for Egypt's over 150 species of birds, such as falcons, vultures, storks, and flamingos, has helped protect their populations.

Sinai's Big Cats

Cats hold a special place in Egyptian culture. In early times, people valued cats for protecting their grain reserves from rats. Ancient people thought of cats as goddesses, and they were afforded many of the same luxuries as humans.

The Sinai leopard, and many of the animals upon which it preys, are protected species in Egypt. In the past, hunters killed the leopard for its attractive hide—this contributed to its decline. Sinai leopards can be entirely black or spotted. Today, protective measures are helping them survive. People are again reporting sightings on Sinai.

These strong, adaptable cats can grow up to six feet in length and stand three feet high. Their range includes different ecosystems across the peninsula, such as desert, grassy plains, and

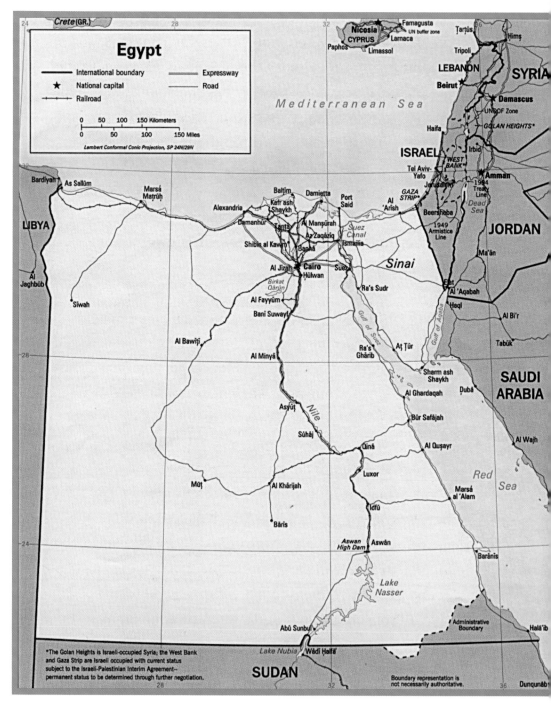

△ A map of Egypt from 1997 showing, among other things, the current borders and major roadways.

mountains. This leopard often feeds on smaller prey, such as gerbils or lizards. Its larger prey includes hoofed animals, such as the ibex or gazelle. It occasionally eats other big cats, like the cheetah. But Egyptian wildlife experts fear the cheetah may be extinct in Egypt; there have been no sightings reported for a decade.[2]

Sinai Environment

The Sinai Peninsula is a land bridge that connects the continents of Africa and Europe. The waters off its coast are also home large marine mammals called dugongs, crocodiles, and snakes. Its land is nearly separated from the rest of Egypt by the Red Sea. The diversity of Sinai's ecosystems attracts millions of people, who come to marvel at its granite mountains and desert dunes, as well as the coral reefs off the coastline.

At the Protected Area of Ras Mohamed at Egypt's Gulf of Aqaba, mangrove forests give way to a marine ecosystem that contains two hundred species of coral. Scientists from Egypt, Israel, and Jordan continuously work together to protect the reef's ecosystem from toxic runoff, waste from ships, and careless scuba divers.

But away from the sea, the Sinai Peninsula contains arid and mountainous environments. Some of the rocks of its highlands are millions of years old. Mount Catherine is Egypt's highest

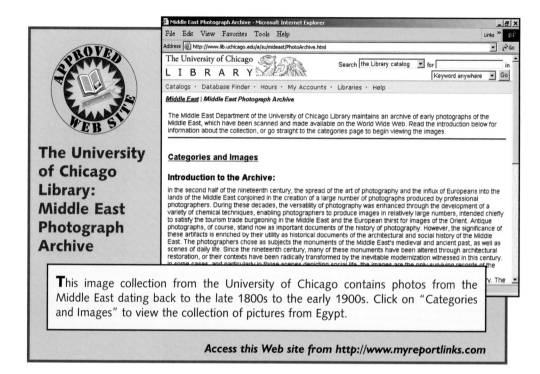

The University of Chicago Library: Middle East Photograph Archive

This image collection from the University of Chicago contains photos from the Middle East dating back to the late 1800s to the early 1900s. Click on "Categories and Images" to view the collection of pictures from Egypt.

Access this Web site from http://www.myreportlinks.com

point at 8,625 feet above sea level. It is also home to an old Christian monastery, which still houses monks today. It officially became an Egyptian Protected Area in the mid-1990s. In these mountains, visitors enjoy spectacular sunsets in pink skies as they leave the park for the night. They can hike on steep mountain trails for awesome views during the day.

Mount Sinai is the spot where followers of the Jewish and Christian religions believe Moses received the Ten Commandments. Sinai attracts thousands of religious tourists each year. It is considered a holy place, because of its rich, biblical history. The Egyptian government is doing its best to make sure humans and wildlife can live together on Sinai.

Protecting Egypt's Environment

Many of Egypt's indigenous animals are housed at the Cairo Zoo. In the past, a wealthy sultan owned the zoo-garden complex, which contains grottos planted with date palms, ferns, and olive and fruit trees, as well as flowers. Some of the same beautiful and fragrant flowers that delighted the ancient Egyptians are thriving here today. These include roses, irises, daisies, jasmine, and poppies. The Egyptian government purchased the zoo a century ago and began to modernize it.

Unfortunately, there are poachers in Egypt who are breaking modern protected species laws. Tourists have reported seeing live and stuffed carcasses of exotic Egyptian animals for sale illegally in Cairo's street markets.[3] In addition, people across the Arab world continue to migrate to Egypt in search of jobs, education, health care, or other benefits. They, too, make demands on the land. Frequent population increases have drained Egypt's natural resources. This has had an impact on its plants and animals.

Tourism Takes Its Toll

In addition to the environmental impact of its residents, tourism affects Egypt's natural resources. In

An Egyptian peasant walks the land with a camel. Camels are among the animals that can be found in Egypt.

summer, Alexandria is a popular travel destination for Europeans and Arabs. People are drawn to Alexandria for its Greek and Roman history, scenic Mediterranean coastline, and cool temperatures, which remain in the 70 to 80°F range throughout the summer season. An urban center, Alexandria is trying to balance commerce with environmental concerns. Generating power and managing waste are among the challenges faced by nearly all Egyptian cities that depend on tourism.

Climate

During the summer, most of Egypt bakes in sweltering 100°F plus temperatures. Thermometers in the western Sahara Desert climb even higher. However, at night, desert temperatures can drop as low as 40°F. When they step away from the camel train and the heat of the campfire, tourists are often surprised to experience cold in the desert. Visitors to Egypt's eastern cities are advised to schedule their trips between November and March to enjoy a more comfortable climate, which may require a light jacket in the morning or evening. However, they are also advised to avoid the storm season, which runs from March to May. For a few months each year, high winds and sandstorms limit outdoor activities across the country.

Egypt is 95 percent desert and most of the country is made of sand. By comparison, Egypt is

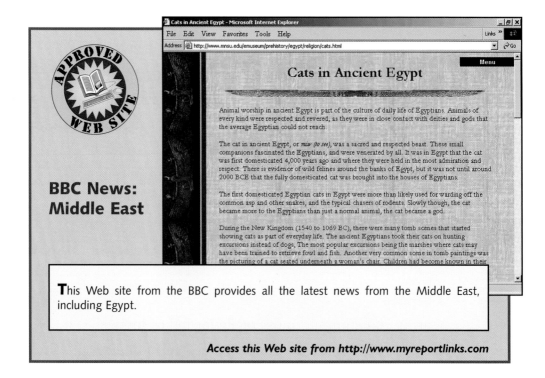

**BBC News:
Middle East**

Cats in Ancient Egypt

Animal worship in ancient Egypt is part of the culture of daily life of Egyptians. Animals of every kind were respected and revered, as they were in close contact with deities and gods that the average Egyptian could not reach.

The cat in ancient Egypt, or *miw (to see)*, was a sacred and respected beast. These small companions fascinated the Egyptians, and were venerated by all. It was in Egypt that the cat was first domesticated 4,000 years ago and where they were held in the most admiration and respect. There is evidence of wild felines around the banks of Egypt, but it was not until around 2000 BCE that the fully domesticated cat was brought into the houses of Egyptians.

The first domesticated Egyptian cats in Egypt were more than likely used for warding off the common asp and other snakes, and the typical chasers of rodents. Slowly though, the cat became more to the Egyptians than just a normal animal, the cat became a god.

During the New Kingdom (1540 to 1069 BC), there were many tomb scenes that started showing cats as part of everyday life. The ancient Egyptians took their cats on hunting excursions instead of dogs. The most popular excursions being the marshes where cats may have been trained to retrieve fowl and fish. Another very common scene in tomb paintings was the picturing of a cat seated underneath a woman's chair. Children had become known in their

This Web site from the BBC provides all the latest news from the Middle East, including Egypt.

Access this Web site from http://www.myreportlinks.com

50 percent larger than the State of Texas. Much of the Egyptian part of the Sahara is considered uninhabitable by humans. However, a small number of Bedouin nomads continue to travel by camel in the desert; their communities are scattered throughout its landscape. In addition, native Berbers live in certain sections of western Egypt. These two groups live in the adjacent desert of neighboring Libya, which is to Egypt's west.

In the western desert, Protected Areas are built around wadis, lowlands that flood with seasonal rains, and oases. These nature reserves allow animals to thrive in their natural habitats in the Siwa, Khargah, Bahriya, Marsa Matrouh, and El Alamein protected areas. Although these areas are sparsely populated by humans, visitors are welcomed by the Egyptians living in these tiny villages among the sand dunes.

Nile Extends for Miles

In the East, water taxis ferry passengers past metropolitan Cairo on the Nile River. People charter boats that travel through the Lower River valley, then up to the Mediterranean Sea. Like any major city, Cairo's population and industries affect the health of surrounding lands and waterways.

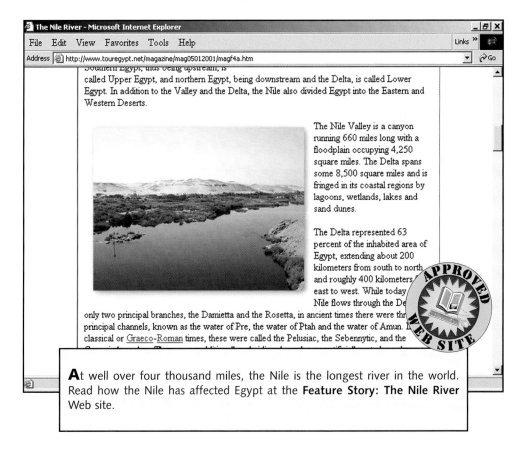

The Nile River – Microsoft Internet Explorer

File   Edit   View   Favorites   Tools   Help   Links »

Address http://www.touregypt.net/magazine/mag05012001/magf4a.htm   Go

called Upper Egypt, and northern Egypt, being downstream and the Delta, is called Lower Egypt. In addition to the Valley and the Delta, the Nile also divided Egypt into the Eastern and Western Deserts.

The Nile Valley is a canyon running 660 miles long with a floodplain occupying 4,250 square miles. The Delta spans some 8,500 square miles and is fringed in its coastal regions by lagoons, wetlands, lakes and sand dunes.

The Delta represented 63 percent of the inhabited area of Egypt, extending about 200 kilometers from south to north and roughly 400 kilometers from east to west. While today, Nile flows through the De

only two principal branches, the Damietta and the Rosetta, in ancient times there were thr principal channels, known as the water of Pre, the water of Ptah and the water of Amun. I classical or Graeco-Roman times, these were called the Pelusiac, the Sebennytic, and the

At well over four thousand miles, the Nile is the longest river in the world. Read how the Nile has affected Egypt at the **Feature Story: The Nile River** Web site.

Irrigation systems extend from the Nile River to outlying areas of its fertile delta for farming. However, a major blow to Egyptian agriculture occurred when the Aswan Dam was completed in 1971. It was originally built to control seasonal floods that made life difficult, or even dangerous, for residents living near the Nile. In this way, it was successful. But the floodwaters had also carried silt, which contained minerals that fertilized the soil on a yearly basis. Without this natural fertilizer, Egyptians have had to find new ways of farming the land.

▷ Ancient and Modern Agriculture

Ancient Egyptians living along the Nile were among the first people to cultivate large-scale crops, such as wheat and hops, from which they also invented bread and beer. People living in the Nile Delta continue their long tradition of farming today. Commercial date farms and cotton plantations are important to Egypt's modern agricultural economy. As in the ancient past, farmers grow figs, carob, dates, olives, and almonds. They also grow flax, garlic, lettuce, onions, and many other vegetables.

Controlling worms and insects that destroy crops is an ongoing challenge for Egyptian farmers. Cotton growers often hire workers to remove by hand leaf worms that destroy plants. In recent years, human rights groups have criticized cotton farmers for hiring children to work long hours in the cotton fields. It is against the law in Egypt and other Arab countries to hire children under the age of twelve.[4]

In the past, growers relied heavily on chemical pesticides to protect their crops. However, this caused toxic runoff problems and threatened plants, birds, and animal species.

Today Egyptians farmers are finding support from their government to create biodynamic all-natural farms to reduce the use of pesticides. The United Nations helped Egypt start this program fifteen years ago. Crop rotation and natural repellents are among the techniques farmers are using as part of the program. At present, there are over one hundred biodynamic farms in Egypt's lowlands.[5]

The Nile River

The Nile River is the longest river in the world, stretching north for about 4,160 miles. The Nile represents life itself to the Egyptian people, ancient and modern.

The Nile River is fed by two smaller rivers: the Blue Nile, which flows into Egypt from the eastern Ethiopian highlands, and the White Nile, which flows from Uganda in the west. These tributaries form the greater Nile River; the two names reflect the color of the water in each. The waters

▲ *These men are working to build a boat along the Nile River.*

of the White Nile are grayer in color, and from a distance, the water appears to be white.

The historic Nile was the subject of a documentary film that was shown in large screen format at theaters throughout America in 2005. *Mystery of the Nile* features a group of adventurers that travels the Nile River by raft and kayak. The expedition begins at the Blue Nile in Ethiopia and ends where the river empties into the Mediterranean Sea. The group encounters many natural and man-made dangers on their journey.[6]

Eastern Egypt is a grid of busy roads that snake across lowlands from city to city. Helwan is located between Cairo and the Suez Canal, which is a major shipping route that connects the Mediterranean and Red seas. El Minya is located on the border between Upper and Lower Egypt. The two names reflect the elevation of the landscape, instead of map or compass directions. Luxor and Giza host tourists from around the world who are attracted to the temples and pyramids.

▶ Life in Lake Nasser

Further south, through Upper Egypt's highlands, is the city of Aswan. It was named for the dam and is located near its reservoir of Lake Nasser. Dugongs live in this lake. The dugong is a species similar to the West Indian manatee found in Florida. Dugongs started congregating behind the

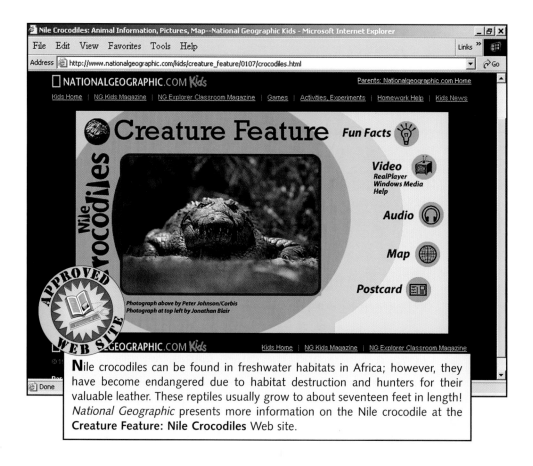

Nile Crocodiles: Animal Information, Pictures, Map--National Geographic Kids - Microsoft Internet Explorer

File   Edit   View   Favorites   Tools   Help   Links »

Address http://www.nationalgeographic.com/kids/creature_feature/0107/crocodiles.html   Go

NATIONALGEOGRAPHIC.COM Kids   Parents: Nationalgeographic.com Home

Kids Home | NG Kids Magazine | NG Explorer Classroom Magazine | Games | Activities, Experiments | Homework Help | Kids News

Creature Feature   Fun Facts

Video
RealPlayer
Windows Media
Help

Audio

Map

Postcard

Photograph above by Peter Johnson/Corbis
Photograph at top left by Jonathan Blair

GEOGRAPHIC.COM Kids   Kids Home | NG Kids Magazine | NG Explorer Classroom Magazine

Nile crocodiles can be found in freshwater habitats in Africa; however, they have become endangered due to habitat destruction and hunters for their valuable leather. These reptiles usually grow to about seventeen feet in length! *National Geographic* presents more information on the Nile crocodile at the **Creature Feature: Nile Crocodiles** Web site.

Done

Aswan Dam after it was built. But the destruction of habitat, as well as hunting, have endangered dugongs' survival in other parts of Egypt. Dugongs also live in the Nile River and the Red Sea; they can live in both fresh and salt water. They can weigh a ton and survive by eating large amounts of sea grass every day. They are genetically linked to land elephants and have similar facial muscles and other physical features. Today, there are laws protecting dugongs in Egypt. It is illegal to hunt them.

Nile crocodiles, one of four African species, also inhabit the waters of Lake Nasser. People hunt them for their tough leather hides. This has contributed to their decline in certain parts of the country. The Nile crocodile can weigh up to 500 pounds, grow up to 20 feet long, and live up to 80 years in captivity. It is ecologically important as a predator. It keeps other predators in check.

Crocodiles prey upon dugongs. They also share the Nile with other large, aggressive animals, like the hippopotamus. Crocodiles feed upon the offspring of these animals when there is opportunity.

Other animals near Lake Nasser include several species of scorpions, cobras and other snakes, and lizards. One of these is the seven-foot-long Nile monitor, Africa's largest lizard. When it feels threatened, the monitor lashes its big tail or bites. It travels on both land and water and can remain submerged in the lake for up to an hour. Other Lake Nasser animal species include the green turtle and birds, such as the white stork, white eye gull, and osprey.

Southeastern Egypt

Southeastern Egypt reflects African life in neighboring Sudan near the base of the Nile. The customs of these people have roots to the ancient Nubians, as well as the Ethiopians still living in the area today. Many Ethiopians are Christians

▲ This is a mud-brick village in southern Egypt. In the south, the way of life more closely resembles other African nations rather than Middle Eastern nations.

the PEOPLE CAllED thEMSElf KEMET

KEMET

BLACK ORIGINAL EGYPTIAN PEOPLE

who perform unique rituals. Ethiopians claim they are guardians of the Ark of the Covenant, which Christians believe contains the Ten Commandments given to Moses on Mount Sinai. An Ethiopian monk continuously guards the holy site containing the ark. No one else is allowed to see it. Today, religious historians are examining possible connections between Ethiopian and Egyptian relics.

E + E = Justice

Chapter 3 ▶

Religion in Egypt

Headline: EGYPT WAGES CRACKDOWN ON RELIGIOUS OUTLAWS

CAIRO – Egyptian police conducted sweeps in spring 2005 that led to the arrest of nearly a thousand people suspected of being members of the outlawed Muslim Brotherhood organization. Today, Egypt continues to hold eight hundred of these people in its jails. These religious fundamentalists have a history of connections to Islamic terrorists.[1]

☆ ☆ ☆

The Muslim Brotherhood organization was formed in Egypt by a schoolteacher nearly a century ago. Members of the Muslim Brotherhood want to make the Qur'an, Islam's holy book, the official constitution of the country. Their idea of a strictly religious government directly threatens President Mubarak, as well as other politicians in the Arab world. For example, in Syria, being a member of the Muslim Brotherhood is punishable by imprisonment or worse. Hundreds of families allege their relatives affiliated with the group have disappeared.[2]

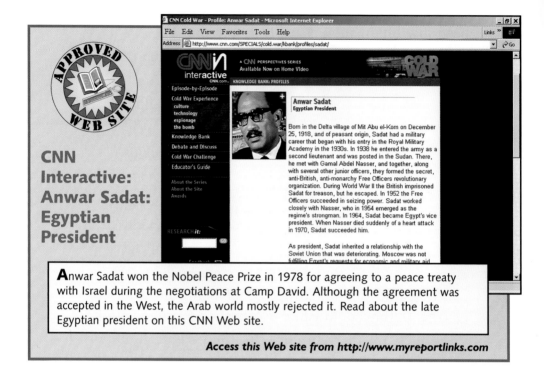

CNN
Interactive:
Anwar Sadat:
Egyptian
President

Anwar Sadat won the Nobel Peace Prize in 1978 for agreeing to a peace treaty with Israel during the negotiations at Camp David. Although the agreement was accepted in the West, the Arab world mostly rejected it. Read about the late Egyptian president on this CNN Web site.

Access this Web site from http://www.myreportlinks.com

In the months following the sweeps, President Mubarak campaigned for his fifth term in office and was reelected. During his campaign, the president told news reporters he was in favor of allowing more political parties to participate in Egypt's elections.[3]

However, the president did not say he would allow members of the Muslim Brotherhood to organize and participate in the election process. President Mubarak is also Muslim. He first took office as Egypt's top leader in 1981 when members of the Organization for Jihad, an offshoot of the Muslim Brotherhood, assassinated President Anwar el-Sadat. This was not the first time the group plotted to kill one of Egypt's leaders. In 1954, members of the Muslim Brotherhood tried to assassinate Egyptian Prime Minister Gamal Nasser. Members from this group had also assassinated Egypt's prime minister five years before the attempt on President Nasser. In response, Prime Minister Nasser, as he was called then, outlawed the organization and jailed its leaders.

In 1964, one of these jailed leaders, Sayyid Qutb, published *Milestones,* a book with strict interpretations of Islam. Today, moderate Muslims claim this book wrongly portrays the Islamic terrorists' idea of jihad to mean a holy war waged on behalf of Islam as a religious duty. Instead, they believe the primary definition of jihad to mean a person's "individual, spiritual struggle against evil. . . ."[4] The author's ideas about declaring jihad on enemies, or perceived enemies, such as the West, influenced Muslim extremists.

Secular or Religious Law

Strict followers of Islam also adhere to separate rules for men and women. Egyptian law does not require women to cover their heads, although many wear the hijab, or head scarf, according to Islamic tradition. Egyptian law is secular; officially, it only applies to state matters, not religious concerns. But in recent years, stricter views of the Qur'an's teachings have taken hold in Egypt.

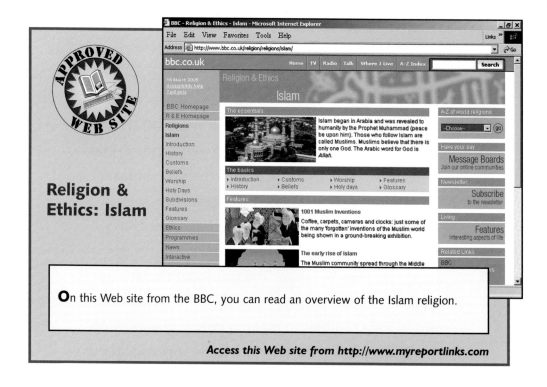

Religion & Ethics: Islam

On this Web site from the BBC, you can read an overview of the Islam religion.

Access this Web site from http://www.myreportlinks.com

Today more Egyptian women are wearing head-scarves to comply with the religious practices of their Muslim families.[5]

Karen Hughes, a United States advisor to President George W. Bush, visited Egypt in September 2005 to meet with Muslim women about improving their civil rights. The response of the group was not favorable to Hughes or United States policy in the Middle East, especially in Iraq. These women accused the United States of bringing more violence to Iraq as the result of waging war there. Many of them wore hijabs and traditional Muslim clothing to this meeting. The women declared that they favored the protections offered by the strict version of Islamic rules that define the roles of men and women in society.[6]

The majority of Egyptians are Sunnis who believe political leaders should be Muslim and are answerable to their people. Like Muslims around the world, Egyptian Sunnis face the holy city of Mecca in Saudi Arabia five times daily to pray. They follow the Five Pillars of Islam. These are rules passed on by the Prophet Muhammad, the founder of Islam, on behalf of Allah, or God.

The Five Pillars

A devout Muslim follows the Five Pillars by declaring allegiance to Allah, praying five times daily, being charitable, and fasting on holy days. One of the pillars is to, at least once, make a pilgrimage to the city of Mecca in Saudi Arabia. This is the birthplace of the Prophet Muhammad. It is also the site of the Al-Haram mosque, which houses the Kaaba, a black structure that houses a rose-colored stone that appears black. Some historians believe the black stone is a meteorite.[7] Some religious followers believe the stone has blackened over time from people's sins.

Muslims ceremoniously circle the stone and kiss it in recognition of its symbolic value as the starting point for devout faith and proper living.

Islam outlines religious rules as to how Muslims are expected to behave during their hajj,

Many consider the Sultan Hassan Mosque in Cairo, Egypt, to be among the most beautiful religious structures in the world.

or pilgrimage to Mecca. Peaceful relations with fellow Muslims on this quest are required inside this holy Muslim city. Non-Muslims are prohibited from entering the holy mosque itself.

Strict Islamists

Some Muslim Brotherhood members say the 1950s marked the end of their use of violence to achieve a strict Islamic society. Yet some members support Muslim extremists fighting against the United States in Iraq and Afghanistan in 2005. They believe their violence is justified in the course of jihad, or the holy war waged against Christians and Jews in the name of Islam.

Egyptian Hassan al-Banna founded the Muslim Brotherhood organization in March 1928, in Ismailiya, a city near the Suez Canal. Hassan preached that Islam is the only correct religion and rejected those who followed Christianity and Judaism. He urged followers to fight Western powers, which dominated several Arab countries at that time.

Al-Banna and those who follow his philosophy believe many things in Western culture violate the teachings of the Qur'an. For example, activities such as dancing are prohibited by strict Muslims. Photographing a woman's face is not allowed. Wine, beer, and other alcoholic beverages are forbidden.

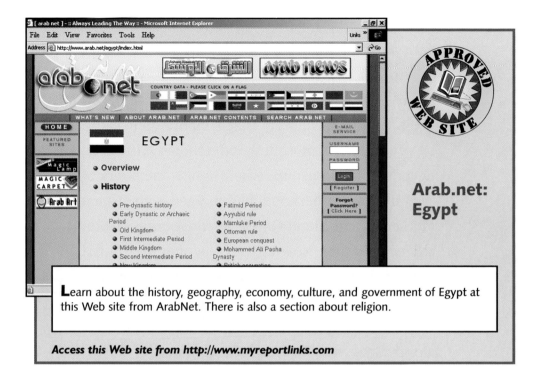

Learn about the history, geography, economy, culture, and government of Egypt at this Web site from ArabNet. There is also a section about religion.

Access this Web site from http://www.myreportlinks.com

Today, some fundamentalists believe Arab political leaders who cooperate with Western governments are against Islam, just as al-Banna did. Thousands of angry Muslims across the globe violently protested when a Danish newspaper published a cartoon depicting Muhammad, their Prophet, with a bomb for a turban (headdress) in 2006. Islamic law prohibits the creation of any images depicting Muhammad or Allah (god).

Many Muslim extremist groups grew out of the Muslim Brotherhood organization; its members combine religion with politics. In the past, they were trained in religion, law, weaponry, and warfare. It has been said that to become an official member, a Muslim man had to take an oath with one hand on the Qur'an and the other on a pistol.[8]

In 2005, the Muslim Brotherhood recognized seven hundred chapters that support their cause by working for mosques and schools. However, Egypt's Al-Jihad group, who are also members of the Muslim Brotherhood, had merged with Osama bin Laden and the al-Qaeda terrorist organization a decade earlier. Now Egypt is helping the United States search for the al-Qaeda members involved in the September 11, 2001, attacks on the United States. Mubarak and other leaders across the world have condemned al-Qaeda's acts of terrorism committed in the name of Islam.[9]

World's First Christians Are Patriots

Coptic Christians are among Egypt's oldest groups. They feel a direct connection to the land, which was home to some of the world's very first Christians. They make up about 5 percent of Egypt's population.[10]

A major difference between the Coptic Christian and Roman Catholic religions is that Copts have their own pope, the Pope of Alexandria and the Patriarch of the Holy See of St. Mark. Orthodox Copts do not recognize the Roman Catholic pope. They will not allow him to hold a holy mass within their monastery's confines.

▲ Members of the Muslim Brotherhood protest the Egyptian government in Cairo. Anti-riot soldiers are in position in case the demonstration turns violent.

However, during Nasser's presidency, Copts have been for the most part excluded from the top posts of the political and administrative bodies of the Egyptian government. Copts regained official stability in Egypt during President Mubarak's terms, although they are still persecuted by extremists. In 2006, the leader of the Coptic Christians was Pope Shenouda III.

Coptic Beliefs

Coptic Christians run over one hundred schools in Egypt. Followers number in the hundreds of thousands. Although they follow the lead of their own pope in practice, some Coptics consider the pope in Rome to be a worthy spiritual leader. The recent visit of the recently deceased Roman Catholic Pope John Paul II to Egypt was a momentous event for these Egyptians. Some began traveling from southern villages to attend the mass several days in advance to secure their spots in the outdoor arena.[11]

Coptic Christians trace their religious roots back to Europe. Another denomination, Coptic Evangelists, have links to America. Today, religious missionaries from this group aid poor Egyptian Christians in their homeland.

Although most Egyptians follow Islam, the government recognizes that Copts are of Egyptian descent. It tries to protect them from Islamic

The Coptic Christians are based in Egypt. This is an image of Coptic priests in Jerusalem taken sometime between 1900 and 1920.

extremists that deny Copts their right to practice Christianity. Generally, thousands of people of different religions across Egypt live side by side peacefully.[12] Its capital city of Cairo is often called a melting pot for this reason.

One part of Egyptian life all of its people share is an ancient religious history. Thousands of years ago, Egyptians believed royalty and divinity were the same. Back then, people worshipped their kings and queens as gods and goddesses. Royalty, in turn, were answerable to higher-ranking gods of the universe. Today, ruins of the temples, tombs, and pyramids built for Egyptian queens and pharaohs rise out of sand dunes toward the heavens.

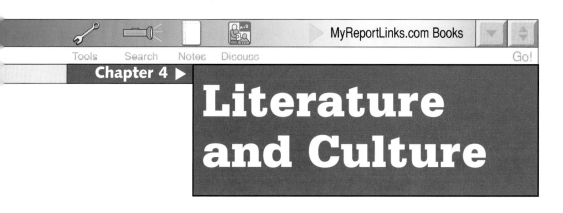

Chapter 4 ▶

Literature and Culture

Headline: MEN HANGED FOR STABBING NOVELIST

CAIRO – Two men were convicted and hanged for stabbing novelist Naguib Mahfouz on the streets of Cairo in 1994. Before his hanging, one of the men admitted he had not read the book he said justified his religiously motivated attack.[1]

★ ★ ★

Naguib Mahfouz, who won the Nobel Prize for Literature in 1988, is a famous author from Egypt. Read his biography on the official Web site of the Nobel Foundation.

Access this Web site from http://www.myreportlinks.com

Mahfouz was awarded the Nobel Prize in Literature in 1988. He is credited with establishing a standard of literature for the modern Arab world. His stories, essays, and poems portray life in contemporary Egypt. A collection called *The Cairo Trilogies* is among his most famous works.

Mahfouz survived the attempt on his life, although he is no longer able to write. He currently lives in Agouza, a suburb of the Egyptian capital city of Cairo. The award-winning author is much beloved among his fellow Egyptian citizens. He highlights ideas about the experiences of everyday Arabs in his stories.

Education in Egypt

Egyptians are credited with one of the world's oldest writing systems, hieroglyphics. Scientists called Egyptologists make careers out of studying these ancient symbols and interpreting their meanings. Later, the Egyptians began writing on small, flat sheets made from a local plant called papyrus. It is thought to have first been used in 4000 B.C.

Education in Egypt is free to its citizens, and school is required for children ages six to twelve. The country is also home to several major universities. Some of them, such as the University of Cairo, are famous centers of Egyptology, the study of Egypt's many civilizations spanning millennia.

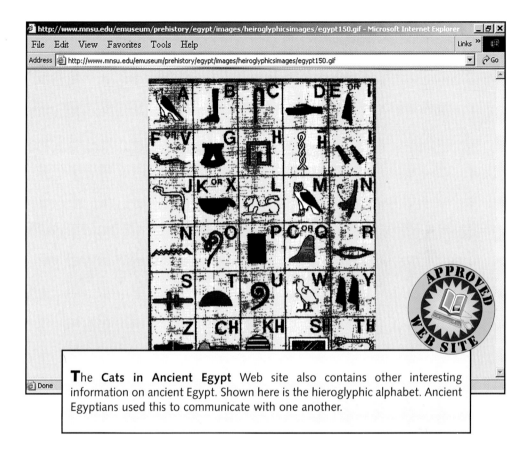

The **Cats in Ancient Egypt** Web site also contains other interesting information on ancient Egypt. Shown here is the hieroglyphic alphabet. Ancient Egyptians used this to communicate with one another.

According to the *CIA World Factbook*, in Egypt, 68 percent of the men and just 47 percent of the women can read and write. Educating children in the western desert, or persuading women from strict Muslim families to attend school, remains a challenge for the government.[2] Egypt's first lady, Suzanne Mubarak, appeared at the opening of a new library in 2005 to encourage people to learn to read.

She and the president's two sons, Alaa and Gamal, were educated in the Middle East and

Egyptian culture is studied throughout the world, and Egypt is home to some of the world's most historic places. The Egyptian Museum, shown here, houses an extensive collection of artifacts from throughout the country's history.

the West. Both of Mubarak's sons are successful businessmen. Recently, Gamal has been outspoken about issues involving Egypt's economy. His opinions have been reported in the Arab news media. Some believe he will be a presidential candidate in the future.[3]

Favorite themes in much of Egyptian literature and theater—and later, in its movies—focus on fantastic moments in a person's life. Some of these include romance, victory over enemies in battle, heroic deeds of Arab tribes, supernatural forces, and dreams. Muslims in Egypt also read books about the Qur'an and poems that reflect the values of Islam. They recite prayers. Coptic Christians read the Bible and the works of their prophets and saints.

Some Muslim children attend religious schools called madrasas in connection with the mosque they attend. These schools typically admit only boys, and lessons focus on learning to recite the Qur'an.

▶ Not Just for Women

Music is a part of everyday life in Egypt. Older, traditional songs in Egypt were about harvests, wars, marriage, work, and daily life. Those who performed songs played instruments, such as violins, harps, or reed pipes. A sistra, or rattle, was used in the worship of Isis, one of the most important goddesses of ancient Egypt. She is one of the only winged deities in Egyptian myth. She is the protector and patron of women. Folk instruments like these rattles continue to be used in Egypt today. Their sound helps traditional dancers maintain rhythm. Companies specializing in Egyptian, Arab, and Oriental instruments are now setting up Web sites to show customers these local products.[4]

Thirty years after her death, singer Umm Kulthoum is still a favorite among Egyptians and other people of the Arab world. Her funeral was the second largest in Egypt's history (President Nasser's was the largest in 1970). Kulthoum won over fans

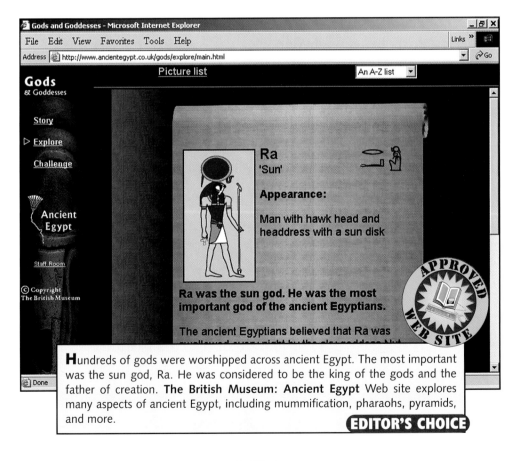

Hundreds of gods were worshipped across ancient Egypt. The most important was the sun god, Ra. He was considered to be the king of the gods and the father of creation. **The British Museum: Ancient Egypt** Web site explores many aspects of ancient Egypt, including mummification, pharaohs, pyramids, and more.

EDITOR'S CHOICE

with her television concerts; at the peak of her career, she presented a new song every month.

Dance in Egypt

In the past, Egyptian men and women danced in lines and performed stories of their culture. Traditional belly dancing, or *raqs sharqi,* was created by Egyptians and included men as participants. Occasions for dance included separate moves for women and men, who usually danced only around people of their same gender. In many cases, acrobatic stunts were incorporated into dancing. Egyptologists discovered drawings of people doing cartwheels while dancing.

Today, belly dancers are almost always women. They continue to perform in Egypt. Some of these dancers are foreigners who come to Egypt to learn about the dance in its homeland. Egyptian belly dancing schools are world famous for their expertise. However, Egyptian belly dancers complain that foreigners take job opportunities away from citizens. For a while, the Egyptian government banned foreigners from working as belly dancers, but it lifted the ban in 2003. Two years later, belly dancers from various parts of the Middle East performed at a convention of dancers in Cairo.

However, many Muslims forbid dancing. They also complain modern, Western-style performers in Egypt move in improper ways and reveal too

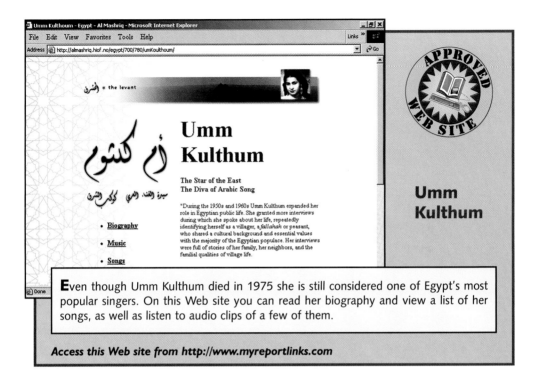

Even though Umm Kulthum died in 1975 she is still considered one of Egypt's most popular singers. On this Web site you can read her biography and view a list of her songs, as well as listen to audio clips of a few of them.

Access this Web site from http://www.myreportlinks.com

much skin instead of covering their bodies. Some Egyptian citizens agree. It is one of the many ways Egyptian society has changed in the past few decades. Newspapers in Egypt often include the opinions of people who reject these modern performers.[5] Egypt's official language is Arabic, although English and French are spoken.

▷ World-Class Taste

Egyptians are accustomed to eating food from all over the world. In Alexandria, for example, cuisine often includes recipes from Europe. Some historians credit Egypt with creating the first pasta, an ingredient usually associated with Italian cuisine.

Many Egyptians dress in a Western style. These women are sitting on the bricks that are a part of the pyramid of Cheops.

Traditional Egyptian food includes a variety of meat and vegetables dishes, along with yogurt, cheese, and sauces. Typical Arab meats are lamb and chicken, but beef, duck, prawns, fish, and even rabbit are grilled or fried based on old Egyptian family recipes. Eggplant, garlic, or chickpeas made into falafel are served with spinach, okra, onions, olives, sweet peas, or jute, a fibrous plant also used to make clothing and rope. Desserts made from dates and almonds, drizzled with honey, are favorite Egyptian treats.

Fashion

It is common for Egyptians to dress up while dining out. Many Egyptians value fashion and invest in the newest styles coming from European and American designers' runways. Historically, Egypt's queens were the models for the country's women. For example, some credit Egypt's Queen Nerfertiti, whose reign dated back to 1300 B.C., with creating a style that combines masculine and feminine qualities called androgyny. Today, men or women who are very thin and wear neutral clothing reflect this style. However, Islam teaches that men and women have separate roles in society that require special dress codes. In strict practice, this could mean a woman must cover her face with a veil.

Another example of the clash between old Egyptian and Islamic tradition involves alcoholic beverages. It is legal to consume alcohol in Egypt, despite some Muslims' objections to it. Ancient Egyptians are credited with inventing wine made from the honey of flowers, which was consumed by its royalty. They also made bread and beer from the wheat and hops they cultivated. Workers who built the pyramids were often provided with, or even paid with, beer.

Social Customs

Today, Egyptians of different beliefs commonly enjoy drinking tea or coffee in city coffee houses. People visit these establishments to socialize, as well as to enjoy treats. Visitors often observe that people in Egypt typically move at a slower pace than do many people in Western societies. While the idea of lingering over tea or coffee has recently become big business in America, it has been a part of Egyptian life for many years.

Throughout the day, Egyptians socialize with friends over snacks or meals, or they browse shops containing locally designed textiles or jewelry. Egyptians are masters of these crafts.

Egyptians learned to grow cotton and became expert weavers. Schools specializing in weaving continue to enroll students from around the world. Egyptians are also excellent jewelry makers; they have had access to diamonds and gems from Africa and Asia for millennia. Egyptian royals adorned

In some of the poorer parts of the country Egyptians use untreated water. This leads to the transmission of harmful diseases.

themselves, their homes, and even their tombs with beautiful clothes, garments, and jewels. Today, many Egyptian people decorate their homes and themselves with mosaic patterns. Repeated shapes and symbols are trademarks of Muslim artwork.

Poor Plagued by Disease

Health problems plague citizens in poor communities. For example, some poor people eat snails from the Nile that are contaminated with worms that then live in the person's intestines. Once the worm enters a body, that person develops severe digestive problems. Many people have died after being infected with this parasite. However, although health care in Egypt is free for citizens, the country does not have enough of the right kind of medicine to cure worm victims. This type of illness has increased in Egypt in recent years.

In some parts of the country, people use water containing harmful bacteria or fail to properly sanitize cooking areas. In the humid climate of the Nile River valley, mosquitoes and other insects carry diseases such as malaria. Today, Egyptians are seeking new technologies to protect health, along with their way of life, which is rich with tradition. The world's first engineers and mathematicians have joined modern nations across the globe in pursuit of solutions for the future.[6]

Chapter 5 ▶

At the Crossroads of History

Headline: KING TUT STILL THE FACE OF EGYPT IN THE WEST

LOS ANGELES – The world's centuries-old fascination with the Egyptian pharaoh Tutankhamen, known as King Tut, continues today in the twenty-first century. King Tut's 3,300 year-old mummified remains and coffin will be on display in four United States cities this year. Technology has

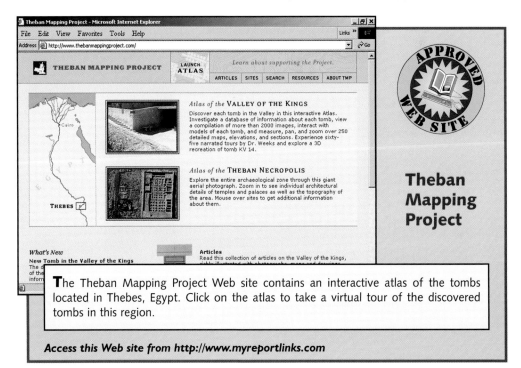

The Theban Mapping Project Web site contains an interactive atlas of the tombs located in Thebes, Egypt. Click on the atlas to take a virtual tour of the discovered tombs in this region.

Access this Web site from http://www.myreportlinks.com

enabled scientists to reconstruct a model of the king's face as part of the exhibit.[1]

✯ ✯ ✯

A mystery still surrounds King Tut's death. Present theories question whether the young king was murdered or died of complications from a broken neck, fractured skull, or a broken leg. Egyptologists continue this debate.[2]

The exhibit featured items not included in the 1970s tour, including the king's royal crown. Westerners, who led the excavations at the site of Egypt's Valley of the Kings after World War I, discovered Tut's tomb and other artifacts. They discovered an assortment of well-preserved items, including gold coins with the king's official stamp on them. King Tut reigned during Egypt's Eighteenth Dynasty.

▶ Periods of Egyptian History

Egyptologists established ways of dividing Egypt's history into time segments. They have identified about thirty royal dynasties and hundreds of rulers during ancient times. Typically, historians identify the Predynastic Period, the Early Dynastic Period, the Old Kingdom, the Middle Kingdom, the New Kingdom, and the Late Period to identify the sequence of Egypt's rulers. In between these time segments are three Intermediate Periods.

The beautifully designed and constructed coffin of Tutankhamen, or King Tut.

The birth of Jesus Christ began a new era in recorded time. The A.D. period, which includes the present day, comes from the Latin words *"Anno Domini."* Latin is an early language spoken in Rome. In English, the words mean, "The Year of our Lord." Empires in Greece and Rome controlled Egypt during the years surrounding Jesus' birth. Their civilizations added this mark in time to Egypt's 365-day calendar. Many people around the world still use this calendar, including Americans.

Inventions and Mysteries

Ancient Egyptians in King Tut's time developed modern technologies still in use, as well. Egyptian inventors began developing ways to collect water and flush waste during the First Dynasty. Thousands of years ago, they built the world's first bathtubs and plumbing systems in Egypt using water from the Nile River.

However, there is controversy among historians as to the identity of Egypt's very first king. The nation's first official leader united the highlands and Nile River Delta areas, called Upper and Lower Egypt. Folklore says Menes was a king who ruled the "Two Lands" nation from the ancient capital city of Memphis. But some archaeologists say Egypt's first king was the ruler of the southern land of Narmer, which then became his namesake.

Some historians have a theory that says King Narmer married a northern princess so people in both Egypt's upper and lower lands would accept his offspring.

Identifying details about the lives of Egypt's kings is an ongoing pursuit for historians from universities around the world.[3]

Over millennia, Egypt's many civilizations continued to make gains. Even though people were born into different social classes, Egyptian leaders afforded them many personal freedoms. People enjoyed long periods of prosperity.

Larger Than Life

The spectacular ruins of the palaces and temples of these civilizations remained long after the kingdoms survived. Sometimes one kingdom added to the grandeur of existing structures. Western archaeologists discovered pyramids and tombs full of ancient treasures thousands of years after they were built. They include the Great Sphinx and monuments in Giza, Dahshur, Zawayet el-Aryan, Saqqarah, and other ruins that still stand next to modern Egyptian cities.

The cities of Karnak, Luxor, and Thebes are among the most frequently visited landmarks in the world. The temples at Karnak were built during the Ramses' reigns. The pharaohs of the eighteenth through twentieth dynasties expanded

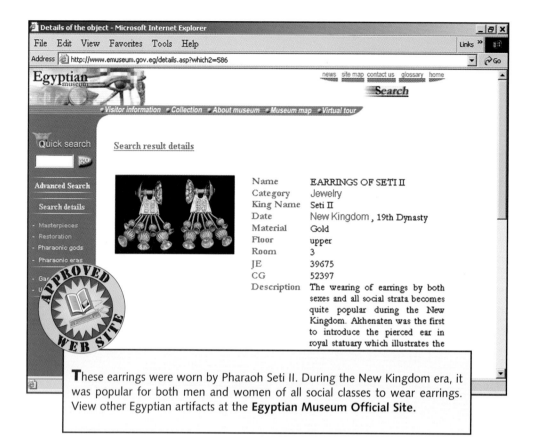

These earrings were worn by Pharaoh Seti II. During the New Kingdom era, it was popular for both men and women of all social classes to wear earrings. View other Egyptian artifacts at the **Egyptian Museum Official Site.**

Karnak during the New Kingdom Period. It became the largest royal complex ever built.

During the Third Intermediate and Late Periods, Egypt's rulers built their monuments outside of Memphis and went instead to Thebes. Inside walls of their temples and coffins are writings contained in the "Book of the Dead." This was a set of so-called magical instructions on how to live in the Underworld, or afterlife, after one had died.

▶ Royalty as Religion

The purpose of the temples and tombs was to give pharaohs a grand send-off to the next incarnation. Their designs demonstrate highly sophisticated mathematical skills. Many also believe the famous Egyptian pyramids, in particular, were built according to the positions of the moon, stars, and sun. This would indicate knowledge of the science of astronomy. The pyramids are the grand tombs of revered Egyptian royals and pharaohs like Tutankhamen.

Because Egyptians thought kings were gods and queens were living goddesses, they believed rulers should take items from earth with them when they died. This is why their tombs are filled with writings, artifacts, and in some cases, jewelry or food. These items would be useful to them in the Underworld.

Belief in an afterlife also prompted Egyptians to preserve dead bodies. The remains of dead bodies were mummified by burying the bodies in hot sand. Later, special substances to embalm the bodies were used, and the bodies were put in decorative coffins. Often, the bodies of prominent Egyptians were laid to rest alongside the mummified bodies of their favorite pets. However, because of their high status in society, Egyptians established special cemeteries for beloved cats.

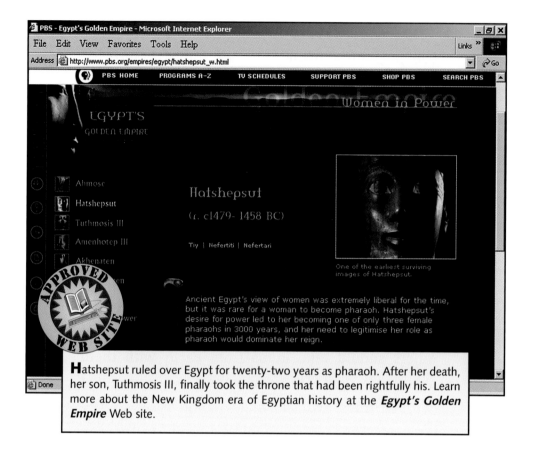

Hatshepsut ruled over Egypt for twenty-two years as pharaoh. After her death, her son, Tuthmosis III, finally took the throne that had been rightfully his. Learn more about the New Kingdom era of Egyptian history at the *Egypt's Golden Empire* Web site.

In summary, ancient Egyptians developed many systems and skills that allowed their civilizations to prosper. For example, they developed many stable sources of food in the Nile River delta. They engineered water systems to grow large-scale crops. They developed ropes to make nets and lines for fishing. They learned how to work with metals to make tools, weapons, coins, and jewelry. Their knowledge of astronomy helped them create a calendar and clocks to measure the seasons and time. They developed a written language.

▷ The Rosetta Stone

The Rosetta Stone is a famous Egyptian artifact. Carved nearly two hundred years before the birth of Christ, it has three forms of writing on it. The first script was the hieroglyphic symbols Egyptians used for important religious documents. The second was the demotic script, commonly used for everyday affairs, and the third was Greek, the language of the nation's rulers.

French soldiers discovered the stone in the delta town of Rashid while rebuilding a fort there in 1799. The stone is named after this town, which translates in English to "Rosetta." A Frenchman familiar with both Coptic and Greek, Jean-François Champollion, was able to decipher the stone in 1822. He determined the stone was written by a group of priests in 196 B.C. to honor their pharaoh, Ptolemy V. This pharaoh's priests issued a series of decrees. The decree were inscribed on stones and erected throughout Egypt. The Rosetta Stone is a copy of the decrees issued in the city of Memphis. The stone includes a number of popular acts, such as reductions in taxes.

Today, enthusiasts enjoy deciphering hieroglyphics for fun. Scientists and historians use them as clues to learn about early Egyptian life. It was common for Egyptian kings and queens to be named after royal relatives who ruled before them. The name Tut in hieroglyphic script is a bird

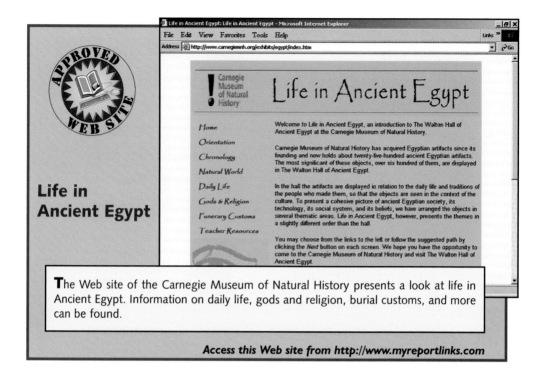

Life in Ancient Egypt

The Web site of the Carnegie Museum of Natural History presents a look at life in Ancient Egypt. Information on daily life, gods and religion, burial customs, and more can be found.

Access this Web site from http://www.myreportlinks.com

between two half circles. The name Cleopatra, the famous queen who ruled during the final Egyptian dynasty, contains several symbols. These include feathers, rope, and human arms with hands. The reign of Egypt's Ptolemaic dynasties ended with her tragic suicide in Alexandria in 30 B.C.

Egypt's Second City

Alexandria is a historical seaport and was the center of Egypt until Muslims built Cairo after A.D. 900. It is named after Alexander the Great, who freed the Egyptians from the Persians, then made himself king. The Persians built the very first canal that connected the Mediterranean and

Red seas. Alexander the Great's Greek influence put King Ptolemy I in power in the Late Period. Ptolemaic kings (who all took the name Ptolemy) often married their sisters and named them Cleopatra, Arsinoe, or Berenice. Their empire fell to Rome after Cleopatra VII's famous romance with Egyptian-born general Mark Antony. The general originally fought for Rome, but then started a war with its leader, Caesar Augustus, known as Octavian. Antony then chose to try to protect Egypt's queen and her people against Rome. After a series of defeats, Antony and Cleopatra fled to Egypt, pursued by Octavian's forces. Finally accepting their defeat, first Antony, then Cleopatra, committed suicide.

Rule of Arab Muslims

Arabs who later converted Egyptians to Islam conquered the Ptolemic empire in 642. Then they founded Cairo, which became the largest city in the region.

Islam solidified its hold in Egypt with the reign of Salah ad-Din, or Saladin, a Kurdish warrior from Tikrit, in Iraq. Saladin was a Sunni Muslim, who defeated the Shi'ite Muslim Fatimid leaders in Egypt in the 1160s. He established the Ayyud regime in Egypt and defeated the Christian Crusaders from Europe in 1192 by recapturing Jerusalem for Muslims. King Richard I of England

Pompei's Pillar is a famous landmark located in the city of Alexandria, Egypt. It is a relic leftover from when the Romans controlled the land that is now Egypt.

had to negotiate with Saladin later to regain a portion of England's former land holdings.

▶ Successful Slaves

The Mamluks were people who came to Egypt as Muslim slaves but then became warriors and rulers. They successfully defeated the Arabs, as well as other invaders. But they also lost Egypt for a time to the Byzantine Empire when the Roman Empire divided. The Mamluks eventually returned to power with the fall of Constantinople in 1453, now the modern city of Istanbul, Turkey. Then Mamluks lost control again, this time to the Ottoman Turks in 1517.

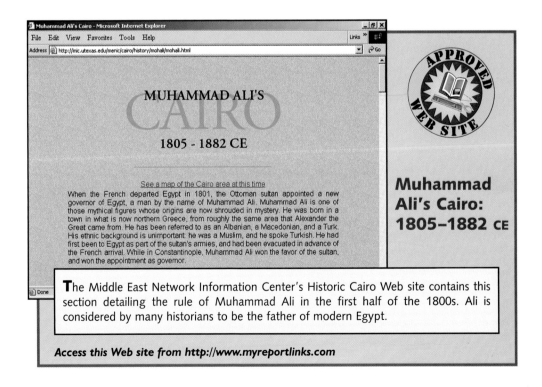

Muhammad Ali's Cairo - Microsoft Internet Explorer

File   Edit   View   Favorites   Tools   Help   Links »

Address http://inic.utexas.edu/menic/cairo/history/mohali/mohali.html   Go

MUHAMMAD ALI'S
CAIRO

1805 - 1882 CE

See a map of the Cairo area at this time

When the French departed Egypt in 1801, the Ottoman sultan appointed a new governor of Egypt, a man by the name of Muhammad Ali. Muhammad Ali is one of those mythical figures whose origins are now shrouded in mystery. He was born in a town in what is now northern Greece, from roughly the same area that Alexander the Great came from. He has been referred to as an Albanian, a Macedonian, and a Turk. His ethnic background is unimportant: he was a Muslim, and he spoke Turkish. He had first been to Egypt as part of the sultan's armies, and had been evacuated in advance of the French arrival. While in Constantinople, Muhammad Ali won the favor of the sultan, and won the appointment as governor.

Done

Muhammad Ali's Cairo: 1805–1882 CE

The Middle East Network Information Center's Historic Cairo Web site contains this section detailing the rule of Muhammad Ali in the first half of the 1800s. Ali is considered by many historians to be the father of modern Egypt.

Access this Web site from http://www.myreportlinks.com

In 1798, General Napoléon Bonaparte of France invaded Egypt and fought the Mamluks at a famous battle at the foot of the Great Pyramid. Here, the French conquered the Mamluk Army. Soon after, British and Turkish soldiers helped Egypt defeat the French. Egypt was again under the control of the Ottoman Empire, which appointed Muhammad Ali as its governor.

During his reign, Ali built roadways and cotton plantations in Egypt, which benefited the economy. But he also killed thousands of Mamluks, many of them during an ambush he staged in the famous Citadel fortress in Cairo. Ali, later called Egypt's Pasha, ruled for three quarters of a century; he died in 1848. Despite his controversial reign, historians credit him with establishing the modern-day Arab Republic of Egypt.[4]

Great Britain occupied the country during World War I. Then Ahmed Farouk, a relative of Ali's, became Egypt's king after Egypt gained some independence from Britain in 1922. The first-half of the twentieth century included a succession of rulers from King Farouk's dynasty. For a time, his kingdom spanned a wide area in the region, including neighboring Sudan.

Egypt's Place on the African Continent

Headline: ETHIOPIA AND EGYPT HOLD NILE RIVER TALKS

SHARM EL SHEIKH – Egyptian president Hosni Mubarak and Ethiopian prime minister Meles Zenawi met in April near the Red Sea to discuss the future of the Nile River's resources. They met

▲ Egyptian president Hosni Mubarak (rights) sits and talks with Ethiopian prime minister Meles Zenawi in Sharm el-Sheik, Egypt on April 17, 2005. The two leaders were discussing how to best utilize the resources of the Nile River.

just prior to the upcoming 2005 Partnership for Africa Summit in Uganda. Nations along the historic Nile River agreed in 1999 to create a new framework for sharing its resources. Currently, Egypt's use of the Nile follows a plan developed by the British nearly a century ago. The agreement between Egypt and Ethiopia will also affect the African nation of Sudan. All of these nations must work together to prosper from the resources of the Nile.[1] Egypt obtains 80 percent of its water from the river.

★ ★ ★

As many as ten African nations share the Nile River's waters: Burundi, the Democratic Republic of the Congo, Egypt, Eritrea, Ethiopia, Kenya, Rwanda, Sudan, Tanzania, and Uganda. In 1959, Egypt signed the Nile Water Agreement with Sudan that shares decision-making power for the Nile River. Thirty years earlier, it had signed a treaty with Great Britain, which gave Egypt control over construction projects and the river's resources.

▷ Best Use of Resources

In 2004, Egypt and its neighbors met in the Ugandan capital of Kampala to discuss dissatisfaction with old water treaties.[2] Some African nations contend that treaties made while Egypt was under European control are no longer valid. These nations are less developed than Egypt. Now they need the Nile's resources for agriculture and to create hydropower for electricity. This will help their communities open businesses and schools and hospitals. Some countries, such as Kenya and Tanzania, are interested in taking water from Lake Victoria, one of the river's main sources.[3]

The British claimed Egypt as a "protectorate" to keep out German forces during World War I. Great Britain's goal was to keep invaders out of the Suez Canal it had helped Egypt build to transport goods. Almost fully independent from Britain

▲ *The British built the Suez Canal to help trade by linking the Mediterranean Sea with the Red Sea. As a result, the British held influence in Egypt for many years. This image of the Suez Canal and Lake Timsah was created between 1856 and 1860.*

by 1922, the Egyptian Parliament implemented a new constitution in 1923. Between 1924 and 1936, Egypt's government was patterned after the European style of government.

During World War II, the Germans successfully invaded Egypt until the British defeated them in the desert at El Alamein, near Alexandria. Land mines still litter the surrounding areas, and local Egyptians warn of the dangers of walking there.[4]

Six months before the end of the war in August 1945, Egypt joined seven other nations in the region to form the Arab League. This was a group of countries that share a common Arab heritage and typically follow the religion of Islam. King Farouk led Egypt at that time. Two decades later, the Arab League formed the Palestine Liberation Organization (PLO). This organization grew under Egypt's control until 1969, when it was taken over by Yasser Arafat, who was born in Cairo. In the years following, the PLO engaged in a campaign of ongoing violence against Israel.

▶ Presidential Approval

One of Egypt's most prominent leaders was Lieutenant Colonel Gamal Abdul Nasser. The son of a postal clerk, Nasser became a soldier, then Egypt's prime minister, then its president, a decade after the war ended. Nasser came to power

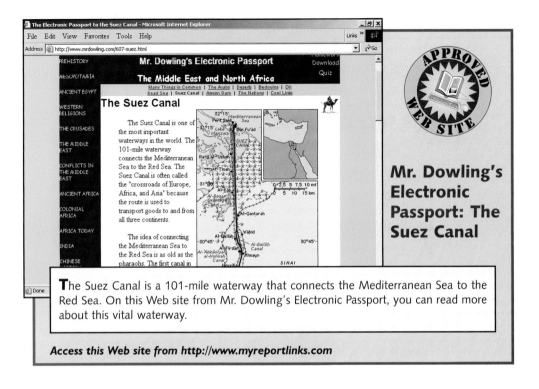

The Suez Canal is a 101-mile waterway that connects the Mediterranean Sea to the Red Sea. On this Web site from Mr. Dowling's Electronic Passport, you can read more about this vital waterway.

Access this Web site from http://www.myreportlinks.com

not long after King Farouk was overthrown. The flamboyant king lost the favor of his subjects. Many did not approve of his habits of eating and drinking to excess, expensive tastes, and disrespectful behavior.

Nasser's mother was ill when he was a boy, so he grew up under the guardianship of an uncle in Cairo. He was famous for looking out for the interests of common Egyptians.[5] For example, when the World Bank and the United States refused to fund the Aswan High Dam project, President Nasser obtained support from the former Soviet Union to build the dam. Such ventures created electricity, jobs, and wealth for the country. Consequently, President Nasser was popular among Egyptians.

The Suez Canal Today

The modern Suez Canal is vital today. The canal connects the Red and Mediterranean seas. The original Suez Canal was an ancient Egyptian waterway. It was the vision of Pharaoh Necho in the sixth century B.C. However, it was under the reign of King Darius I that the canal was first completed. It consisted of two parts. One linked the Red Sea to the Great Bitter Lake; the second linked the lake with a branch of the Nile River.

The Canal served as a route between Europe and India. It was re-dug during the Roman rule around A.D. 100, then re-dug again six centuries later. It fell into disrepair after the Europeans discovered ways around the African continent. French engineers spent eleven years excavating the modern Suez Canal in the late nineteenth century, opening it for the first ships in 1869.

France, Britain, and Israel seized control of the Sinai Peninsula and other parts of Egypt in 1956. Egypt considered Israel an enemy during this time period. A year later, Egypt boldly reoccupied the Sinai, and the United Nations persuaded Israel to withdraw. This gained President Nasser much favor among his proud people. In the twenty-first

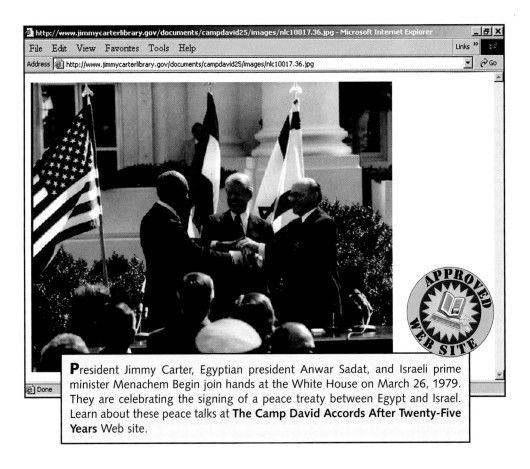

http://www.jimmycarterlibrary.gov/documents/campdavid25/images/nlc10017.36.jpg - Microsoft Internet Explorer

File   Edit   View   Favorites   Tools   Help   Links »

Address http://www.jimmycarterlibrary.gov/documents/campdavid25/images/nlc10017.36.jpg   Go

Done

President Jimmy Carter, Egyptian president Anwar Sadat, and Israeli prime minister Menachem Begin join hands at the White House on March 26, 1979. They are celebrating the signing of a peace treaty between Egypt and Israel. Learn about these peace talks at **The Camp David Accords After Twenty-Five Years** Web site.

century, the Suez Canal is patrolled by international forces and remains a major trade route.

In 1967, Israel took the offensive and seized the West Bank from Jordan and land along the Mediterranean Sea, the Gaza Strip, from Egypt.

President Nasser died of a heart attack in 1970. His fierce devotion to Egypt made him an icon among his people.

Vice President Anwar el-Sadat was elected president following President Nasser's death. He had met President Nasser at the Royal Military

Academy Sandhurst, in England, when Egypt was under British control in the 1930s. They later served in the military in Sudan. However, after Nasser's death, Sadat would spend his life reversing his friend's government policies.

Upon taking office, President Sadat distanced Egypt from the Soviet Union and mended relations with the United States. He opened elections, granting citizens more opportunities to participate in government. A devout follower of Islam, President Sadat accepted the influence of the Muslim Brotherhood organization for a time. Once again, resentment increased among Egyptian Muslims against the Jewish people of Israel. Egypt and Syria attacked Israel in 1973.

Five years later, President Sadat met with United States president Jimmy Carter and Israeli prime minister Menachem Begin to sign the treaty that was the result of the famous Camp David Peace Accords in the woods of Maryland. President Carter helped the two nations form a peace treaty that remains in effect. As part of the treaty, Israel officially returned Sinai to Egypt.

▶ Sharing the Nobel Peace Prize

The two Middle East leaders shared the Nobel Peace Prize for signing the accord. But angry members of the Arab League expelled Egypt for making peace with Israel. At home, President Sadat's "open government" and alliance with Muslims backfired, as Islamic extremists became openly hostile toward him. President Sadat was assassinated by Islamic extremists on October 6, 1981, while watching a military parade.

Hosni Mubarak, Egypt's current leader, was then elected president. Mubarak's many challenges include maintaining peace with the international community and protecting Egypt from terrorists. The Arab League welcomed back Egypt in 1989 under President Mubarak's leadership.

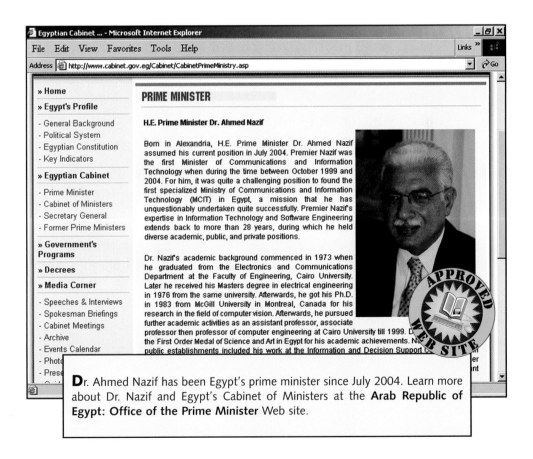

Dr. Ahmed Nazif has been Egypt's prime minister since July 2004. Learn more about Dr. Nazif and Egypt's Cabinet of Ministers at the **Arab Republic of Egypt: Office of the Prime Minister** Web site.

Today, President Mubarak is being pressured from foreign supporters, as well Egyptians, to change the nation's political structure. Western powers that support Egypt with economic aid want Mubarak to increase personal freedoms and democracy. Many citizens want the same. However, strict Muslims in Egypt want a government that more closely follows Islamic law, called Sharia.

The Arab Republic of Egypt now has twenty-six governorates, which are similar to American counties. Its legal system is based on a combination of English law, Islamic law, and French codes. The Egyptian Supreme Court and Council of State oversees the decision making of administrators. Its executive branch includes President Mubarak, Prime Minister Ahmed Nazif, and Cabinet members, who are appointed by the president.

In May 2005, Egypt's government passed a constitutional amendment that changed the format of Egypt's presidential elections to allow multiple candidates. Previously, Egypt's president was nominated by a group called the People's Assembly and approved by a national referendum. However, there remains a ban on religious-political parties, which prohibits leaders of extremist groups from running for government office.

Chapter 7 ▶

Is Egypt Positioned to Prosper?

Headline: HARD TIMES FOR EGYPT'S TOURISM INDUSTRY

GIZA – In Egypt it is customary for travelers to negotiate fares with taxicab drivers. Haggling is simply part of doing business.[1] But the practice only benefits drivers when the numbers of customers is greater than the number of available

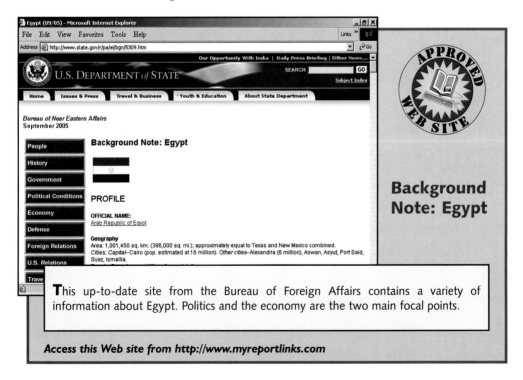

This up-to-date site from the Bureau of Foreign Affairs contains a variety of information about Egypt. Politics and the economy are the two main focal points.

Background Note: Egypt

Access this Web site from http://www.myreportlinks.com

taxicabs. Drivers only profit when tourists are creating a demand for their services.

The number of foreign tourists has declined in Egypt in recent years in the wake of violence.[2] Today the country is trying to attract tourists from the Arab world, which make up only one fifth of total visitors to Egypt each year.[3] Whether people who depend on Egypt's tourism industry, such as taxicab drivers, will prosper in the coming years is uncertain.

☆ ☆ ☆

▶ Traveling about Egypt

To hail a taxi in Egypt, a person stands at the side of the road and calls out the destination. When a driver stops, he will make a deal with you about the cost of the ride. Travelers report that even though sometimes the mileage meters do not work, there are rarely problems once a fee is set.

Recently, competition for business has increased among taxicab drivers. This benefits riders more than drivers. Also, shuttles are available at Egyptian airports that offer flat rates to popular destinations.[4]

Another inexpensive way to get around in Cairo is to take underground metro trains. Trains operate from early morning to midnight to shuttle 2 million tourists and business people daily. French and Japanese engineers built the Cairo metro lines. They were the first underground trains in Africa and the Middle East. They are clean and generally efficient, with only occasional delays.[5]

Although tourism makes up less than 10 percent of Egypt's economy, it has been a reliable source of revenue for many years. People from all over the world dream of traveling to Giza and Luxor to marvel at the temples and pyramids built by ancient pharaohs. Thousands wander the museums of Cairo, an international hub, or the shores of Alexandria, rich with dramatic history, each year. Nile River cruises continue to delight modern adventurers. Wildlife enthusiasts enjoy sightings in the Sahara or on the Sinai Peninsula or scuba dive at the Red Sea. Now economists

Egypt State Information Service: Your Gateway to Egypt

This Web site from the government-run Egypt State Information Service provides extensive information on this Middle Eastern country. Find out about Egypt's land and people, history, politics, economy, and more.

EDITOR'S CHOICE

Access this Web site from http://www.myreportlinks.com

wonder whether these unique destinations will continue to lure vacationers to the site of the world's oldest civilizations.

Tourism Suffers

Today, violence in Egypt and throughout the region is keeping tourists away. The tourism industry has suffered the side effects of political unrest in Egypt for the past decade. The car bombings at a Red Sea resort in summer 2005, which killed sixty-four people, have added to tourists' concerns about safety. The terrorists who waged these attacks somehow made it through checkpoints set up along the roads leading to Sharm el-Sheik.

The Egyptian government and travel agencies report tourism has declined since 1999, the most profitable of the past ten years. This affects thousands of Egyptians who rely on the nation's tourism industry for income. The unemployment rate in Egypt is approximately 15 percent. Some eight hundred thousand job seekers look for work here annually.[6]

The International Monetary Fund (IMF) provided financial support to revitalize tourism in Egypt after the attack in 1997 on Luxor. But economic reforms, such as the move toward privatization, fell short of foreign expectations. The financial support agreement with the IMF has since expired. Now pressure is on President Mubarak to open Egyptian markets to private competition.[7] Some Egyptians are putting pressure on the government to decrease its involvement in business or deregulate Egypt's industries. Foreign investors have urged the Egyptian government to increase opportunities for private companies to sell goods and services.

Bankers and Berbers

Egypt's economy is the second largest in the Arab world, second to oil giant Saudi Arabia. Income comes from Suez Canal tolls, tourism, agriculture, textiles, capital investments, foreign aid, workers' foreign income, and hydrocarbon exports. The Egyptian pound (LE) has proven to be a stable currency in the world market. In the 1990s, Egypt reformed its banking system to more closely model that of the United States. Although Egypt's Central Bank controls the value of the nation's currency, private, specialty, and even foreign banks can choose the fees they charge customers. Private banks in Egypt are also free to offer services that increase their business.

Petroleum production in the Gulf of Suez accounts for 50 percent of Egypt's oil exports. The Sumed Pipeline was built under the water of the Suez Canal for this oil complex. These structures help Egypt transport Arab oil to Europe. Egypt

An Egyptian guide at the Pyramids of Giza.

exports some of its own crude oil to Asia. Its main trading partners are the United States, Italy, Germany, Japan, and South Korea. Ultimately, the Suez Canal helps Egypt compete in the global market.

Recent natural disasters in the United States and in different parts of the world have resulted in increasing demands for oil. In addition the fast-growing economies of China and India have needed more oil. Yet Egypt is not a member of the Organization of Petroleum Exporting Countries (OPEC). This is a group of nations that control gas prices. The Egyptian government sets its own prices and often purchases oil on the market for use within its own borders.

Natural gas deposits in the Nile Delta and Egypt's western desert are beginning to brighten the outlook for the nation's economy. In 2005, Egypt signed an agreement with neighboring Israel to build a natural gas pipeline between the two countries. Two years earlier, a pipeline was completed that extends from El Arish in Egypt to Aqaba in Jordan. This opened natural gas trade between these Arab neighbors.

Center of Commerce

The Cairo Stock Exchange is internationally recognized as the center of commerce in the Arab world. Egyptian businessmen also run many of the

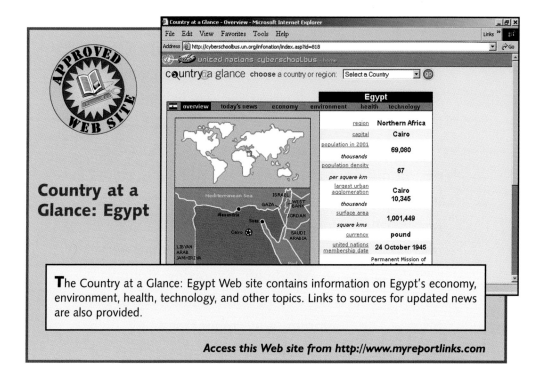

Country at a Glance: Egypt

The Country at a Glance: Egypt Web site contains information on Egypt's economy, environment, health, technology, and other topics. Links to sources for updated news are also provided.

Access this Web site from http://www.myreportlinks.com

corporations that provide construction workers and contractors, oil refining and exporting services, telecommunications products, and transport and shipping services. Many successful Egyptians attend prestigious business schools abroad and then return home on an Egypt Air jet to invest in Arab markets.[8]

In recent years, Egypt has increased mining operations for minerals such as phosphates, rock, and iron ore. But this pursuit must be weighed against its impact on the environment, which includes farming. Agricultural products comprise 15 percent of the nation's economy. In addition to crops, livestock—such as horses, camels, and sheep—help stabilize this industry.

Finally, Egyptian economists are not ready to abandon profits from tourism.

An emerging industry called ecotourism could also enhance the economy. This involves bringing guests on wildlife-viewing safaris. Protected areas, such as the Siwa oasis in the Sahara, may bring business to native Egyptians such as the Berbers.

There are 50 million Berbers across Egypt and northern Africa. Originally, they inhabited larger areas of North Africa. Thousands of years ago, Egypt enjoyed a wetter climate and the soil was more fertile. Berbers fled to the Sahara to

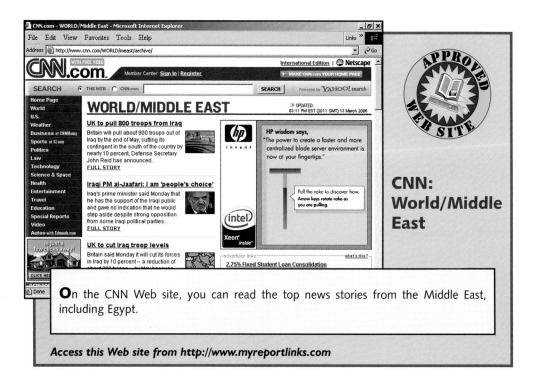

CNN: World/Middle East

On the CNN Web site, you can read the top news stories from the Middle East, including Egypt.

Access this Web site from http://www.myreportlinks.com

escape persecution and imperial conquests by foreign invaders. Today most have converted to Islam.[9] They have become adept at living in the harsh desert and they are familiar with wildlife there. Knowledge of the terrain, plus their ancient history, could be used to attract tourists to Berber communities in 2005. However, this will likely require investments from wealthy Egyptians or the government. The Berbers trace their ethnic roots back to 3000 B.C., the beginning of recorded history.

The population of Egypt is estimated to be 100 million by 2050.[10] This means the nation will need more schools, hospitals, housing, and electrical power. Currently the Aswan Dam generates nearly 20 percent of the nation's power. Besides becoming a leading export, natural gas holds promise as an energy source for Egyptians at home.

Chapter 8

Egypt's Children Compete in the Modern World

Headline: EGYPT WINS FIFTH AFRICAN CUP OF NATIONS SOCCER TOURNAMENT

CAIRO – Egypt's Pharaohs soccer team won its fifth African Cup of Nations title yesterday in a penalty shot against the Ivory Coast Elephants. Across the country, Egyptians cheered their team to victory on February 10, 2006, in Cairo.

Security was tight at the tournament. Last year, cup officials visited Cairo Stadium to determine whether renovations could make it a secure event site. They also visited neighboring cities to examine facilities for both athletes and spectators.

Egypt is confronting new waves of terrorist attacks and violence related to political unrest. More recently, it is struggling with near chaos on its border near the Gaza Strip. In fall 2005, the Egyptian government announced it would accept help from European troops in guarding its border there.

Promoters of the African Cup say that advertisers sought assurances that Egypt would be able to protect people during the event. The timely completion of repairs and preparations were also of concern to organizers. They feared Egyptian bureaucracy could cause delays. Anxieties escalated in 2005 after Egyptian Football Association

Like many other Middle Eastern nations, soccer is a very popular sport in Egypt. In 2006, the Egyptian soccer team won the African Cup of Nations tournament for the fifth time and Ahmed Hasan, an Egyptian player, won the competition's Best Player Award. Read about the Egyptian soccer team at **The Official Site of the Egypt 2006 MTN Africa Cup of Nations** Web site.

(EFA) President Samir Zaher expressed concerns about the nation's state of readiness for the games.[1] Four Egyptian cities hosted the celebrated tournament, including Alexandria.[2]

✯ ✯ ✯

Soccer, or football as it is called across the world, is the most popular sport in Egypt. Passion for this sport reflects the nation's international profile. Egyptian youths enjoy playing with friends or in leagues, as well as rooting for their national teams when the games air on television. There is competition among fans for tickets to big games.

Some say that a form of football originated in ancient Egypt in about 2500 B.C. Some historians believe Egyptian men courted women by competing on the football field, or pitch. However, in 1848 the British drew up the first set of rules for what became the modern game of football. British soldiers and government officials, spread the game across Europe, Asia, Africa, South America, and the Middle East during British rule in those areas.[3]

Education for Egypt's Youth

Thousands of Egyptian youths sneaked away from their chores or studies to watch the game on television. Egyptian families are feeling the financial strain of educating their children. They need money for uniforms, books, and other fees. Some people feel compelled to send their children to private schools in the hopes of obtaining the best education for them. As the demand goes up, tuition for private schools continues to increase. Many parents wonder whether public school is an acceptable alternative.[4]

Arab people from the region flee to Egypt to escape their homelands. This puts more children in Egyptian classrooms. Some public school classes have as many as seventy students enrolled in them. Public school teachers in Egypt are poorly

▲ On February 3, 2006, a ferry carrying 1,400 people caught fire and sank in the Red Sea. The young man in the center is distraught because his father was among the passengers that were still missing the following day.

paid. Many supplement their incomes by tutoring students after school hours. While many students would appreciate help with homework after school hours, often their families simply cannot afford tutors' fees.[5]

Some parents travel to other parts of the region to find work as laborers. But being away from their families is a hardship. In early 2006, thousands of workers drowned when an Egyptian ferry sank in the Red Sea. Whether the tragedy was caused by the poor condition of the ship or bad weather or both, it is under investigation. Citizens expressed frustration when the Egyptian government did not communicate the status of rescue operations in the hours that followed.

Religious Schools

There are other concerns about the education of modern Egyptians. Some Muslim families prefer religious schools that focus on the teachings of Islam. Usually, only boys attend these schools. This fundamentalist religious movement is gaining momentum in Egypt. Children who wander the desert as Bedouins, or live in remote villages like the Berbers, do not always have access to schools. In the future, limited educational skills will lead to limited opportunities for employment. This means people will need Egypt's government to take care of their needs.

Lack of education can also lead to poor health choices. Even though health care is free, people cannot obtain the medicine they need to treat illness, or are unaware of how to prevent disease. Land mines scattered across Egypt often claim children as victims. Some lose their lives, while others lose their hearing, eyesight, or limbs.[6]

Finally, surrounding countries want to use natural resources like the Nile River.

Now Egypt is under pressure to share control of these resources while trying to meet the needs of its growing population. It has formed agreements with other nations in the region during the past five years to build natural gas pipelines as a source of energy and income for the country's economy.

In September 2005, President Mubarak called upon the United Nations to hold an international antiterrorist conference. He delivered his speech shortly after the UN adopted two resolutions. One outlines the UN Security Council's role in preventing conflicts.

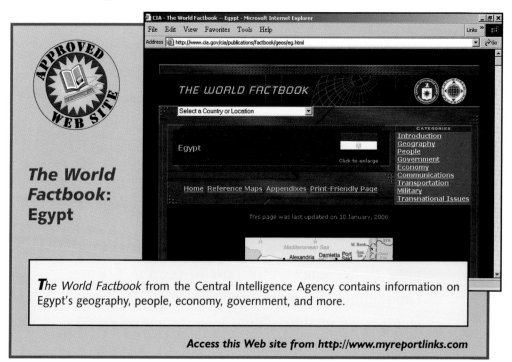

The World Factbook: Egypt

The World Factbook from the Central Intelligence Agency contains information on Egypt's geography, people, economy, government, and more.

Access this Web site from http://www.myreportlinks.com

The other condemns the attempt of any group to justify terrorist acts or incite further attacks.

Egypt, one of the oldest civilizations on earth, is at the crossroads of the African continent and Middle East. Today the Arab Republic of Egypt is at a turning point its own modern history.

Report Links

The Internet sites described below can be accessed at http://www.myreportlinks.com

▶**The World Factbook: Egypt**
Editor's Choice Learn more about Egypt from this CIA Web site.

▶**The British Museum: Ancient Egypt**
Editor's Choice Learn about ancient Egypt from this British Museum site.

▶**Perry-Castañeda Library Map Collection: Egypt Maps**
Editor's Choice View historical and present-day maps of Egypt.

▶**Egypt Daily**
Editor's Choice Get the daily news from this Egyptian news Web site.

▶**Egypt State Information Service: Your Gateway to Egypt**
Editor's Choice Get all the information you need about Egypt on this government Web site.

▶**Embassy of Egypt (Washington DC)**
Editor's Choice Read more about Egypt from their U.S. Embassy Web site.

▶**Arab.net: Egypt**
This Web site provides a general overview of Egypt.

▶**Arab Republic of Egypt: Office of the Prime Minister**
Learn more about Egypt's Cabinet and the office of the Prime Minister.

▶**Background Note: Egypt**
Travelers to Egypt should check out this site from the U.S. State Department.

▶**BBC News: Middle East**
Get the latest news from the Middle East.

▶**The Camp David Accords After Twenty-Five Years**
Learn more about the Israeli-Egyptian peace talks at Camp David.

▶**Cats in Ancient Egypt**
This site looks at the role of cats in Ancient Egypt.

▶**CNN Interactive: Anwar Sadat: Egyptian President**
Read about Anwar Sadat, the president of Egypt from 1970 to 1981.

▶**CNN: World/Middle East**
Read the latest news from Egypt and the Middle East.

▶**Country at a Glance: Egypt**
Find information on Egypt on the United Nations Web site.

Report Links

The Internet sites described below can be accessed at
http://www.myreportlinks.com

▶**Country Profile: Egypt**
The BBC provides an overview of this Middle Eastern country.

▶**Creature Feature: Nile Crocodiles**
Learn more about the Nile crocodile from this site.

▶*Egypt's Golden Empire*
Take a look back at the New Kingdom era of Egyptian history on this site.

▶**Egyptian Museum Official Site**
Explore the collection of the Egyptian Museum in Cairo.

▶**Egyptian Presidency**
Read about the current president of Egypt, Hosni Mubarak.

▶**Feature Story: The Nile River**
Learn more about the longest river in the world.

▶**Life in Ancient Egypt**
Learn more about life in Ancient Egypt on this Web site.

▶**Mr. Dowling's Electronic Passport: The Suez Canal**
Learn about the 101-mile Suez Canal on this Web site.

▶**Muhammad Ali's Cairo: 1805–1882 CE**
Read about Muhammad Ali, considered the father of modern Egypt.

▶**Naguib Mahfouz: Biography**
Read about this Nobel Prize winning author.

▶**The Official Site of the Egypt 2006 MTN Africa Cup of Nations**
Read about the Egyptian soccer team and the 2006 Africa Cup of Nations.

▶**Religion & Ethics: Islam**
Learn more about the Islam religion.

▶**Theban Mapping Project**
Take a virtual tour of the famous area known as the "Valley of the Kings."

▶**Umm Kulthum**
Learn about this very popular Egyptian singer.

▶**The University of Chicago Library: Middle East Photograph Archive**
View photos from Egypt and other Middle Eastern regions.

Aswan Dam—Dam built from 1898 to 1902 in an effort to aid farming along the banks of the Nile River. Named after the town of Aswan, that is on the banks of the Nile.

Bedouin—A nomadic people who live in the deserts of the Middle East and North Africa.

Berbers—Tribal people living in North Africa that trace their roots back to the beginning of recorded history.

biodynamic—A way of farming that uses only organic materials.

Copts—Members of the Coptic Christian church which is based in Egypt.

Cradle of Civilization—A name given to parts of North Africa and the Middle East where the first humans were thought to have developed societies.

dugong—A sea mammal similar to a manatee, that is also called a sea cow.

Egyptologist—One who studies ancient Egypt.

embassy—The official home of ambassadors living in a foreign country.

extremists—Those who have or support extreme political or religious views.

Gaza Strip—Stretch of land in the Middle East bordering the Mediterranean Sea and Israel. Palestinians consider this to be part of their homeland. Egypt controlled it from the end of World War II until they lost it to Israel in 1967. Israel returned it to the Palestinian people in 2005.

Hamas—Palestinian political party and militant group. Some countries, such as Israel and the United States, consider Hamas to be a terrorist organization.

infidel—Someone who does not believe in the majority religion.

Luxor Temple—A temple located in the city of Luxor, which is along the Nile River in South Egypt.

Muslim Brotherhood—An extremist group in Egypt that wants the Egyptian government to be strictly ruled by Islamic law.

natural gas—A type of fuel that is found in the earth's crust in some places.

Pyramids of Giza—Ancient Egyptian graves that have become a popular tourist destination. They are also among the oldest manmade structures in the world.

sandstorm—A desert windstorm that stirs up intense clouds of sand.

Sharm el-Sheik—A resort community on the Sinai Peninsula.

Shi'ite—A member of the Shi'a sect of Islam, who believe that only descendants of Ali are the rightful leaders of Muslims.

Sinai Peninsula—Egyptian peninsula located between the Mediterranean Sea and the Red Sea.

Six-Day War—An Arab-Israeli war that took place in 1967. At the conclusion of this war, Egypt lost control of the Gaza Strip.

Sunni—A sect of Islam that believes the first four caliphs are the rightful leaders of the Muslims.

wadi—Streambeds that have water during the rainy season, but are dry the remainder of the year.

Chapter 1. Egypt Protects Centuries of Progress

1. Associated Press, "Al Qaeda in Iraq: Egyptian Envoy Killed," *FoxNews.com*, July 8, 2005<http://www.foxnews.com/story/0,2933, 161782,00.html> (July 5, 2006).

2. Emily Wax, "Egypt pleads for kin but bars martyrs," *Sydney Morning Herald,* April 7, 2003,<httP://www.smh.com.au/articles/2003/ 04/06/1049567566141.html> (July 6, 2006).

3. Bureau of Democracy, Human Rights, and Labor, "Country Reports on Human Rights Practices," *U.S. Department of State,* February 28 2005, <http://www.state.gov/g/drl/rls/hrrpt/ 2004/41720.html> (July 6, 2006).

4. MASNET and News Agencies, "Rice in Egypt Calls for Democracy," *Muslim American Society*, June 20, 2005, <http://www.masnet .org/news.asp?id=25387 (July 6, 2006).

5. Bureau of Democracy, Human Rights, and Labor, "Country Reports on Human Rights Practices."

6. CNN/Reuters, "Egypt could lose U.S. trade deal if talks delayed," January 18, 2006.

7. Ashraf Sweillam, "Egypt Explosion Injures Two Canadians," *abcNews International*, August 15,2005,<http://abcnews.go.com/Internationl /wirestory?id=10389777> (July 6, 2006).

8. United Nations Security Council press release: SC/6170, "Security Council calls on Sudan to extradite suspects in attempted

assassination of Egyptian president," January 21, 1996. <http://www.un.org/news/Press/docs/1996/19960131.sc6170.html> (July 6, 2006).

Chapter 2. Egypt's Land and Climate

1. *Haaret* and *Jerusalem Report,* "Israel and Egypt Sign Natural Gas Deal," *Jewish Virtual Library*, July 1, 2005, <http://www.touregypt.net/featurestories/cats.htm>(July 6, 2006).

2. Mark Hunter, "The Greater and Lesser Wild Cats of Egypt," *Tour Egypt,* n.d., <http://www.touregypt.net/featurestories/cats.htm> (July 6, 2006).

3. Tortoise Trust, "Report on Inspection Visit to Saiyyida Aisha Market Cairo," June 1997, <http://www.tortoisetrust.org/activities/cairo.html> (July 6, 2006).

4. Human Rights Watch, "Underage and Unprotected: Child Labor in Cotton Pest Management," February 11, 2006, <http://www.hrw.org/reports/2001/egypt/Egypt01-05.htm#P204_35669> (July 6, 2006).

5. UN Department of Economic and Social Affairs, "Application of Biodynamic Methods in the Egyptian Cotton Sector," *Division for Sustainable Development*, 2000, <http://www.un.org/esa/sustdev/mgroups/success/SARD-27.htm> (July 6, 2006).

6. Orbita Max and MacGillivary Freemen documentary film, *Mystery of the Nile*, IMAX Corporation, 2005.

Chapter 3. Religion in Egypt

1. Ashraf Sweillam, "Egyptian Police Fight Gunbattles, Storm Militant Strongholds in Sweep for Bombing Suspects," *NCTimes.com*, August 24, 2005, <http://www.nctimes.com/articles/2005/08/25/news/nation/16_38_058_24_05.txt> (July 6, 2006).

2. Scott Peterson, "How Syria's Brutal Past Colors its Future," *The Christian Science Monitor*, June 20, 2000, <http://www.csmonitor.com/2000/0620/pls3.html> (July 6, 2006).

3. Dan Murphy, "Egypt Keeps Muslim Brotherhood Boxed In," *The Christian Science Monitor*, September 27, 2005, <http://www.csmonitor.com/2005/0607/p01s04-wome.html> (July 6, 2006).

4. Muqtedar Khan, "A Fresh Look at Sayyid Qutb's *Milestones*," *IJTIHAD: A Return to Enlightenment*, <http://www.ijtihad.org/sq/htm> (July 6, 2006).

5. Casual Cairo detours, "Frequently Asked Questions," n.d., <http://www.casualcairodetours.pyramids.net/faq.html> (July 6, 2006).

6. Charles Wolfson, "Karen Hughes' Trip to Egypt," *CBS News.com*, September 26, 2005, <http://www.cbsnews.com/stories/2005/09/27/politics/main887324.shtml> (July 6, 2006).

7. Jack Wheeler, "Moses in Mecca," *Freedom Research Foundation*, October 10, 2000, <http://www.newsmax.com/archives/articles/2000/10/10/145501.shtml> (July 6, 2006).

8. Murphy, "Egypt Keeps Muslim Brotherhood Boxed In."

9. *The Egyptian Gazette On-Line,* "Egypt welcomes SC motions on terror and conflict prevention," September 16, 2005, <http://www.algomhuria.net.eg/gazette/1/> (July 6, 2006).

10. Frank Gardner, "Who are Egypt's Christians?" *BBC News,* September 27, 2005, <http://www.news.bbc.co.uk/1/hi/world/middle_east/653574.stm> (July 6, 2006).

11. Ibid.

12. ArabNet, "Religion," 2002, <http://www.arab.net/egypt/et_religion.htm> (July 6, 2006).

Chapter 4. Literature and Culture

1. Lawrence Wright, "The Man Behind Bin Laden," *The New Yorker,* September 16, 2002, <http://www.newyorker.com/fact/content/?020916fa_fact2a> (July 6, 2006).

2. *Sudan Tribune,* "Egyptian first lady opens library in Hurghada," August 25, 2005, <http://www.sudantribune.com/article.php3?id _article=11274>.

3. Arabic News.com, "Egypt's Economic Picture is not Dim," May 10, 2000, <http://www.arabicnews.com/ansub/Daily/Day/000510/2000051056.html> (July 6, 2006).

4. Tehuti Research Foundation, "Egyptian Musical Instruments," *Rediscover Ancient Egypt,* September 12, 2004, <http://www.Egypt-tehuti.org/books/musical-instruments.html> (July 6, 2006).

5. Heather Sharp, "Sexy Stars Push Limits in Egypt," *BBC News*, August 4, 2005, <http://news.bbc.co.uk/1/hi/world/middle_east/4722945.stm> (July 6, 2006).

6. Tore Kjeilen, "Egypt Health & Education," *Encyclopaedia of the Orient*, 1996–2006, <http://lexicorient.com/e.o/Egypt_3.htm> (July 6, 2006), and Schistosomiasis Control Initiative, "What is Schistosomiasis?" *Imperial College London*, n.d., <http:// www.schisto.org/schistosomiasis/> (July 6, 2006).

Chapter 5. At the Crossroads of History

1. Paul Zemanek, "Pharaoh's Farewell," *Southwest Airlines Spirit Magazine*, June 2005.

2. Ibid.

3. Jimmy Dunn, "Who Was Menes?" *Tour Egypt*, n.d., <http://www.touregypt.net/featurestories/menes1.htm> (July 6, 2006).

4. Yunan Labib Rizk, "The Assumption," *Al-Ahram Weekly On-Line*, Issue 737, March 24–30, 2005, <http://weekly.ahram.org.eg/2005/735/chrncls.htm> (July 6, 2006).

Chapter 6. Egypt's Place on the African Continent

1. Gamal Nkrumah, "Nile Basin Countries re-double efforts to work out a way of sharing and managing the region's water resources," *Al-Ahram Weekly/Yale Global Online*, June 11, 2004, <http://yaleglobal.yale.edu/display.article?id=4080> (July 6, 2006).

2. Ibid.

3. Ibid.

4. Arabic News.com, "Egypt plagued with 22.7 million landmines," June 23, 2000, <http://www.arabicnews.com/ansub/Daily/Day/000623/2000062344.html> (July 6, 2006).

5. Central Intelligence Agency, "Egypt," *The World Factbook*, June 29, 2006, <http://www.cia.gov/cia/publications/factbook/geos/eg.html> (July 6, 2006).

Chapter 7. Is Egypt Positioned to Prosper?

1. Jimmy Dunn, "Getting Around in Cairo," *Tour Egypt*, April 1, 2001, <http://www.touregypt.net/magazine/mag04012001/magf3.htm> (July 6, 2006).

2. Paul Garwood, "Egypt Expects Quick Tourism Recovery," *San Francisco Chronicle*, July 24, 2005, <http://www.sfgate.com/cgi-bin/article.cgi?f=/n/a/2005/07/24/financial/f151231D9O.DTL> (July 6, 2006).

3. BBC News, "Uganda 'draining Lake Victoria'," February 9, 2006, <http://news.bbc.co.uk/2/hi/africa/4696240.stm> (July 6, 2006).

4. Dunn, "Getting Around in Cairo."

5. Ibid.

6. Agence France Presse (AFP), "Egypt makes tackling unemployment a priority," *The Daily Star,* January 31, 2006, <http://www.dailystar.com.lb/article.asp?edition_id=10&categ_id=3&article_id=21831> (July 6, 2006).

7. Edward S. Walker, "Mubarak's Challenge," Middle East Institute report, April 12, 2004.

8. Central Intelligence Agency, "Egypt," *The World Factbook*, June 29, 2006, <http://www .cia.gov/cia/publications/factbook/geos/eg .html> (July 6, 2006).

9. Tore Kjeilen, "Berbers," *Encyclopaedia of the Orient*, 1996–2006,<http://lexicorient .com/e.o/berbers.htm> (July 6, 2006).

10. Central Intelligence Agency, "Egypt."

Chapter 8. Egypt's Children Compete in the Modern World

1. AllAfrica.com "Egypt 2006 Under Scrutiny," October 2, 2005, <http:// allafrica.com/stories/200509190520.html>.

2. Ibid.

3. Ibid.

4. Bureau of Near Eastern Affairs, "Background Notes: Egypt," *U.S. Department of State*, September 2005, <http: //www.state.gov /r/pa/ei/bgn/5309.htm> (July 6, 2006).

5. Ibid.

6. Arabic News.com, "Egypt plagued with 22.7 million landmines," June 23, 2000, <http://www.arabicnews.com/ansub/Daily/ Day/000623/2000062344.html> (July 6, 2006).

Aykroyd, Clarissa. *Egypt.* Philadelphia: Mason Crest Publishers, 2004.

Bramwell, Neil D. *Ancient Egypt: A MyReportLinks .com Book.* Berkeley Heights, N.J.: MyReportLinks .com Books, 2004.

Broyles, Matthew. *The Six-Day War.* New York: The Rosen Publishing Group, 2004.

Cheshire, Gerard and Paula Hammond. *The Middle East.* Broomall, Pa.: Mason Crest Publishers, 2003.

Hobbs, Joseph J. *Egypt.* Philadelphia: Chelsea House Publishers, 2003.

Parker, Lewis K. *Egypt.* New York: Benchmark Books/Marshal Cavendish, 2003.

Pateman, Robert, and Salwa El-Hamamsy. *Egypt.* New York: Benchmark Books/Marshal Cavendish, 2004.

Rivera, Sheila. *Women of the Middle East.* Edina, Minn.: Abdo Publishers, 2004.

Rosenberg, Aaron. *The Yom Kippur War.* New York: The Rosen Publishing Group, 2004.

Whitehead, Kim. *Islam: The Basics.* Broomall, Pa.: Mason Crest Publishers, 2004.

———. *Islamic Fundamentalism.* Broomall, Pa.: Mason Crest Publishers, 2004